edition lichtland

© Birgit Medele

edition Lichtland
Stadtplatz 4, 94078 Freyung
Deutschland

Gestaltung: Edith Döringer
Satz: Melanie Lehner

1. Auflage 2012

ISBN: 978-3-942509-24-4
www.lichtland.eu

Birgit Medele

*An initiation
 into the art of letting go*

Clear your Clutter

Manifest your Dreams

Acknowledgements

I would like to thank:
My husband, the love of my life
Our wonderful children
My parents, siblings and friends
All those who contributed their experiences, questions and insights (thanks Christine)
My editor Lilias Martin and the publishing team at Lichtland
All those who inspire me through the way they live/d
Life itself

Contents

Preface 11
I Clearing as personal development 16
II Why we find it difficult to let go 22
    Suppress emotions 22
    Feign security 24
    Create identity 26
    Do the 'right' thing 28
    Act out inner rebellion 34
    Keep options open 37
III Clearing as an art of living 40
    Bye bye prejudice 41
    Letting go without regret 44
    Make those decisions 48
    Take responsibility 50
        Appreciate our unique journey 51
        Energy management as self-management 53
        The art of accepting 56
    Refurbish relationships 61
        The art of letting be 61
        Setting boundaries 66
    Become aware 71
        Clarity and vision 71
        Equanimity 76
        Intuition 82
        Patience and self-discipline 84

IV Clearing secrets revealed: where to start
and how not to stop! 87
    Fine feathers make fine birds 96
    Conquering the paper mountains 104
    The desk reborn as an oasis of calm 107
V Mental Clutter 115
    Thoughts that take us round in circles 115
    Time management – the end of a myth 119
    Putting off procrastination – once and for all! 124
    Multi-tasking – the end of another myth 127
    Electronic clutter 128
VI Emotional Clutter 132
    Pointless feelings 133
    Patent remedies 140
VII Staying afloat 145
    The art of not-buying 145
    Clutter hide-and-seek 149
    Living life to the full 151

    Bonus track
    The Feng Shui Bagua 156

Preface

Dear reader,

Cupboards crammed, desk piled high, head bursting? You are not alone. On average we own about 10,000 things, most of which we never use. This stuff quite literally burdens us. The good news there is a cure for wanting to buy ever more objects to clog up our home and life. Decluttering lightens our load, being organised is the most underrated shortcut to happiness. "Yes, I know", you are mumbling now. "But somehow I never get round to making a start. Or I stop, exhausted and overwhelmed, after about five and a half minutes." Why? The answer is hidden in the realms of energy.

You know how decluttering works, in theory. You do not need a book to tell you how to organise your cutlery drawer. What you are after is the motivation to get going and here is what you were waiting for: a written pep talk! *Clear your Clutter* brings you an energy supply vast enough to see you through the first half hour of decluttering and then the next and the next. A practical guide that throws open a few cabinet doors; takes a closer look at the stuff that drops onto our head and examines the symptoms of our passion for collecting. What are we trying to store in our drawers, shelves and boxes? Joy, laughter, adventures, inner peace? Often we resort to hoarding stuff in order to get closer to life itself.

Clutter clearing is never about things. It is not about time either, this fleeting something that comes dressed up in hours and minutes and never hangs around long enough to give us a chance to clear the decks. Clearing is not even about struggling with the memories related to our every thing. It is all about energy. Clinging to objects when we can no longer offer them a meaningful life is draining. We banish them to linger in the nirvana that is spare rooms and loft spaces, waiting for a brighter future, the redemption day of decision-making that never comes. Not for them, not for us.

Being disorganised throws us off balance and turns us into one of those absent-minded, lethargic beings we were determined never ever to end up as. Owning too much exhausts. It distracts from mapping out the next goal, from finding meaning in being.

Why can we not let go? Let's explore the contents of kitchen cupboards and under-bed storage and find out what our stuff is all about. We are fed up with choosing all the time; between 15 varieties of jams and conditioners and customised coffee – grande skinny decaf double shot anyone? We need a break from having to get it right, forever forced to filter relevant data from the dross. It is tiring to worry about missing out, to live in fear of making a wrong decision – should I have chosen strawberry flavour instead?

This book volunteers as a companion for navigating the contemporary information-overload-jungle we tend to get ourselves lost in. It digs out the signposts that have been overgrown by piles and gigawatts at some remote point in time. It maps out a path off the beaten track, away from the superfluous towards the truly good stuff, the deep-down desires that got buried underneath our lovely clutter a long time ago.

You might have put off the odd clearing project. "I'm going to sort through the attic, the sock drawer, the paperwork as soon as I find the time." Yeah, right! Does this sound familiar? We will never make time as long as we continue to misconceive decluttering as a drag. Why not give the good old clearout a break, have another look and discover its inherent beauty. Clearing is so full of promise, all glittering and sparkling on the inside; no exception here, the inner qualities are those that count. Let's do it justice at last and rebrand organising as a master class in life skills, an archaeological expedition of a different kind that entices us along on a journey. Instead of digging through pyramids we delve into our own history which is just as exciting and nerve-wracking. We lay bare our past, get back to our roots, while working our way through harmless enough looking stacks of paper. Memories and feelings come flooding in. Clearing is a stripping away of the inessential that helps us cut through the excess to the emotions and desires buried underneath. Assisted by long forgotten possessions, we get acquainted with ourselves all over again. Objects serve as witnesses and we are the leading star in a detective story, trying to establish how that magic flame inside got suffocated by the clutter gang.

Decluttering is not about getting rid of everything. It is about sorting through belongings to achieve a more comprehensive understanding of ourselves. What feels good, what feels right, what has become a burden?

Clutter clearing is more holistic than yoga and meditation put together and the most powerful Feng Shui tool you could wish for. We can while away the hours rehanging mirrors and programming crystals or simply shrink our To-do-list. Hearts and minds clear and open up in an environment that feels spacious, bright and airy.

Getting organised is personal development. It is a journey towards more energy, clarity and joy. Make it into a game, go through closets, chitchat and certificates, unburdening on all levels. Chuck the freed up boxes into the river of life, hop onto the makeshift dingy, set sail and take off towards the next laugh, the next discovery!

Clearing frees up emotional space, it allows for filling this very moment with as much joy as we can cram into it. It transforms us and our surroundings. We stop drifting, break free from the golden cage that our home has become and turn it into the mast of a yacht. Pointless routines go overboard, anchors aweigh, hold on tight and off into an effervescent, raffish life that does not use up all available energy to just, somehow, get through yet another day. Instead we are cruising along with abundant vitality supplies, enough to care about ourselves and others. It brings within reach a life that allows for lighting up eyes. For a moment. For a day. Forever!

In the unlikely case that this has yet to convince you – you are still reading, or are you already furiously busy *sorting things out?* – just think of decluttering as shopping in reverse! Items found by my clients include cash, crates of wine, jewellery, antique coins, birth certificates, gift coupons and parking vouchers, art materials, stamps and stationery, long lost contact details. You name it, they found it. You too can discover tons of things you forgot you had, imagine the joy: all this new stuff, without spending a penny. Who would want to go shopping if they could get digging?

Our surroundings drain or recharge us. How can you spot a feel-good oasis? It reflects who you are, is easy to maintain and supports you in your priorities. If your home or work environments do not meet those criteria at the moment –so much the better. The tiniest positive change in our living space has a direct impact on our life. It feels so wonderful to let go of excess stuff because the purification on the outside also frees the self. Decluttering is a holistic detox.

Welcome to the magical world of the clearout, the Sesame-open into a wonderful lightness of being.

I Clearing as personal development

What is the most thrilling thing about things?

Their stories. Every single item tells a unique tale of memories, plans, hopes or dreams. We use objects as props in the theatre of our life. When the stage gets too crammed, performers find it increasingly difficult to manoeuvre. No plot can unfold if the actors keep tripping over random stuff. The art of living is about keeping only those props around us that assist us in reaching our goals. If we never clear the stage, we will find ourselves rehashing outdated plays and ancient dramas over and over. The present literally needs space to unfold; scope for meaningful growth and progression.

Imagine you are the director in charge of putting on a new play: a brand new phase of your life; another crisp, unique, as yet untouched morning. What if you have to work on a stage that still features every single prop of all past shows? What are your chances of creating something new? If we apply that analogy to our home or workplace, how much future can we fit in? Any evidence of the present? Everything crammed to the hilts with the past? Inherited furniture, pictures, vases, presents, cards and souvenirs of the last decades; baby pictures of the children who moved out a long time ago. Homes have a tendency to turn into museums over time. Before we know it, we live in a sarcophagus, an archive, a storage unit of times gone by. If we have just celebrated our 98th birthday and love sitting down in an armchair to look at gently yellowing photo albums, this does not bother us at all. However, if we are still full of plans and beans and have a few years left to reach that age, the stagnation manifested in our museum surroundings does not help.

Tackling the problem zones gets trickier over time. We are energetically connected to our home. Congestion on the level of objects mirrors an overall energy blockage. Matter vibrates, as the physicists explain. We are flickering on and off fast enough to be able to lounge on moving atoms, blissfully unaware of the micro-particles zooming around that happen to form a sofa for us at this point in time. Intuitively however, we do register these vibes. It is no coincidence that we instantly feel upbeat or at peace on entering a building or room; that we enjoy staying in certain spaces. Good vibrations. Elsewhere we would rather turn on our heel and walk out again. Every object has an impact on our heart and soul. If we surround ourselves with things that have a joyful vibration, the environment feels like that – swinging, come rain or shine.

When does an object have joyful vibrations? When it is loved and used. A book was born to be read. Banned on a shelf to collect dust, dog-eared and lonely, it is as good as dead and emits sad 'nobody loves me' frequencies, turning the corner from book to burden before our very eyes. Enter the secret daydreams of gentle burglar fairies that would flutter past to lighten our load, clear out the wardrobe, relieve us of the dreaded decision making and gift us with a fresh start and the insurance money. Expats have admitted to hopes that their overseas container would miraculously disappear and sink into the remotest depths of the oceans. For the same reason the thought of a holiday appeals, preferably far away. All we have to drag with us are two (or five) suitcases, the responsibility for the rest of our stuff stays at home.

Less is more has become a cliché, a retailers' mantra to make us buy their storage 'solutions'. It still rings true though because objects can be demanding. They hurl themselves at us in a never-ending chorus of silent requests. "Look at me. Carry me back to where I live. Oh, actually, I don't have a permanent residence yet. Can't you allocate me one, right now? Please? And then tidy me away? Organise me. Notice me. Enjoy me! Alright then, at least put me out of sight somewhere." Things are begging for attention, relentlessly. They want to be listened to, leafed through or, even worse, read properly. They need dusting, washing and ironing, folding, wrapping, unwrapping. They want to be carried upstairs and then downstairs again. Protected from cold, heat and moths and stored in a cool dry place. Admired, handled and sorted, ideally alphabetically. Cleaned, glued back together, sewn on, rearranged, filed, fixed, dusted, donated. Constantly they come up with new ideas. "Find me. Shred me. Didn't you mean to sell me? I am past my use by date, dispose of me – in an ethically responsible, environmentally friendly and politically correct way, of course. Have you put me on the insurance, by the way?" Their never-ending nagging unnerves us. We are trying hard not to listen. Very hard. And on they go. "Buy more boxes, baskets, filing cabinets for us, another chest of drawers would come in handy or how about a trunk? Don't forget to rent additional storage space and protect us with a safe and burglar alarm. Why not leave the car in the rain and let us live in the garage?" Finally they urge us to build an extension or move to a bigger place. "We need more space." They put us through the paces, not a moment's rest or relaxation until they have been dealt with. "No time right now, later," we sigh, rushing on. The sheer presence of unwanted objects is exhausting because we never seem to be able to cater to their infinite needs. One client summed it up brilliantly, "They just sit there and look at you accusingly."

Less *is* more. Our stuff, however, could not care less about this truism and continues to multiply. Somehow word must have got out that we loved cats and before long we are inundated with kittens in every conceivable shape and form: ornaments, mugs, wall calendars and kitchen towels, pens, mousemats, the works. They move in without a rental contract and then miraculously manage to resist eviction. We are just sitting there, minding our own business and then the mail comes in, the bargains and special offers and all those bothersome bits and pieces that require us to make decisions about them. We do not feel like making a decision at the moment, tomorrow we will take action on the annoying flatmates that take over more and more of our precious space. For now we could do with a rest, thank you very much. Meanwhile the relentless piles turn into mini-mountains, get banished into storage boxes while more unwanted stuff creeps in. The spare room fills up, space is running out in both loft and garage and we never seem to get round to doing that car boot sale…

Clutter is everything we do not use or love and anything unfinished. It can be a piece of paper that is past its useful-by date or a habit that we have outgrown. Clutter is stuck energy that makes us prisoners of the past and blocks good new things from coming into our lives.

We are connected to everything we own. Welded to it, hardwired through invisible energy spaghetti no matter where on the globe we deposit our stuff. We are dragging every single teaspoon with us wherever we go, every spare nail, screw, pencil stub and paper clip. The entire contents of shed and loft are connected to us on an energy level. We lug them around, soundlessly clanking and rattling with every motion. As long as the spaghetti strings are attached in a somewhat organised way we are still able to move. The more we get entangled, the more exhausting it becomes to negotiate the next 48 hours. The following exercise illustrates this.

Briefly close your eyes and connect to your bed. In your mind, try to locate the latest electricity bill, the door keys, a pair of scissors, a piece of string. Finding your bed was straightforward enough, you knew exactly where it was. Locating the other items was probably slightly more interesting as you had to mentally hunt around until you managed to track them down. The longer it takes to make a connection, the more muddled up the energy-spaghetti. The longer our to-do list, the more challenging it becomes to wade through the morning into the afternoon. It feels so good to devise an organising system or get something done because we do not have to invest energy into constant unravelling. We can head straight towards our goals instead of having to negotiate homemade hurdles.

Decluttering has been getting a bad rap as allegedly one of the most unglamorous, some even say boring activities going. Think again. The most fascinating philosophical and psychological concepts are right in there, take your pick. Which life skill would you like to test drive first: learn to say no, develop your intuition, become more patient? Withdraw into the cosy, securely limited space of a cardboard box and start to practice the big stuff: dealing with transience and death, growth and new beginnings... Explore your wellbeing, your life, your journey through clearing out your clutter. How does that sound? Life coaches charge for their services, boxes never do!

Here is a story for you. A tourist on a walking holiday had been looking forward to a guided tour through a mountain monastery. Now the big moment has come. She tiptoes into the cell of a monk and looks around for a while. "May I ask you something?" The monk smiles "Of course." – "Where are all your things?" The reply is a counter question. "May I ask you something?" – "Go ahead." – "Where are all *your* belongings?" "Well, I'm obviously just travelling through here?"

You can guess the reply.

Clearing checks us out of the 'Apathy Inn'. We get to unearth unexploited potential under layers of stuff; scramble over the props and head for the truly fascinating territory that unfolds behind the scenes. Crack open the first box to embark on a journey of self-discovery towards a creative life full of drive and enthusiasm.

II Why we find it difficult to let go

Clutter clearing is an exploration where we encounter the psychology of why we find it hard to throw stuff out. Coming up: a selection of possible reasons for a refusal to let go – some might be familiar, others will not tick any of your boxes. Have fun digging!

Suppress emotions

Chaos theory is not a theory, it manifests as everyday experience. Our things lead lives of their own, gallivanting all over the place, driving us mad with their unsettledness. Instead of staying put on the desk, paper starts trekking through the house to grow roots in the most ridiculous places. After a frantic game of hide and seek, we track the bill down: it had gone underground in a shoe box in the kitchen cupboard. Magazines, books and toys for all ages multiply over night. Getting the wardrobe doors to shut is a workout far superior to any gym session and by the time we successfully prise them open again, we do not fancy wearing any of the stuff crammed in there.

Organised clutter lovers take pride in arranging their unused belongings, whiling away the hours meticulously folding, filing, labelling, rearranging and folding some more. Kept busy with the administration of stuff they rummage through their days, limiting themselves to the relatively straightforward question of where do I store this? Hypnotised by the steady rhythm of constant shifting – up down, in out, down up, left right – there is no time for pausing or reflecting. We get sidetracked playing in our life-sized Wendy house full-time, plodding along in a comfy illusion of being busy and therefore important and needed. It is easy to mistake movement for achievement and get fooled by being forever busy – doing what? The most useful side effect of this mock activism in our hamster-wheel home is that we never have to sit down and face an empty moment. We avoid unoccupied time and the confrontation with questions lingering right underneath those boxes, ready to jump at us. "Why are you here, what are your dreams? How can you fulfil your potential? Where to from here?" Clutter is a protective device, a skilfully constructed obstacle course that keeps out the intruders that we cannot simply file away. Clutter is a wall that we erect between us and the scarier topics. It keeps them at bay, we take the foot off the accelerator and grind to a halt in our bagged up comfort zone. Diligently beavering away, we set up a dam to stem the floods of feelings: the longing for a partner or the career change we never embarked on. Grief for the children we never had, loved ones we lost, opportunities missed. Sadness that the children we did have stopped being children and have moved out, moved on and left us. We try to fill an inner void with stuff, plaster over the hurt with yet another purchase.

The root cause for a passion for collecting can be hidden in the past. Perhaps our ancestors lost their belongings when they had to suddenly leave a city or country. Wander back in time: when did the hoarding start? Was it after a separation, divorce or bereavement, a traumatic childhood experience? One day you might have come home from school to find that a favourite soft toy – the rocking horse or train set – had disappeared. Your guardians had decided that, "You didn't need that anymore." You had been ignored and hurt. Deeply. Ever since, you have been trying to fill the gap caused by this wound; never letting go of anything; holding on to a boxed-up, past out of sight but not out of mind. At some point it became impossible to pluck up the courage to wake the sleeping memories. As long as the cartons are dozing, sealed and untouched, we do not have to deal with our stuff. We create a protective shell, an additional layer between us and the world out there or the worlds inside ourselves. Clutter is a cocoon. It tones down life; holds it at bay, shoved into some sort of receptacle. Stick on the label, fasten the lid; sorted. Those shielding mechanisms temporarily make sense, but after a while the disadvantages become obvious.

In a cocoon you cannot see very far. Only once we break free, can we emerge as the iridescent butterfly that we really are and set off, gently tumbling towards our dreams.

Feign security

Too many of our bits and pieces get an easy ride when it comes to the crunch-question: should it stay or should it go? They pass the acid test with the eternal favourite of all hoarder excuses, "That might come in useful one day!" Even if we don't need it, the children might want it in fifteen years time. Or a friend. The neighbours..? Underneath this innocent little excuse lurks a paralysing emotion; fear. We might have been spared first-hand experiences of hunger or homelessness, but still catch ourselves humming along to the feeling tones of an ever-present subconscious 'tomorrow there might not be enough.' Maybe some of our predecessors had to endure war times or an economic depression. Poverty consciousness can be passed down through the generations, but we can break the chain and transform fear vibes and cultivate trust every time we let go of an object that was kept incarcerated in a box dungeon for security reasons only. Once we have realised that our expectations create our reality we unsubscribe from the widespread mantra, "Every time I give something away I need it again". Instead we use the brand new confidence gained from clearing successes (five pairs of trousers, three chipped mugs, one flaky friend!) to pat ourselves on the back and say out loud, "Should I ever require a spare tin opener again, I trust life will provide me with an even better one." Using objects as security blankets is a habit we can break anytime we choose to. For a child, pieces of fabric transform into an imaginary friend and we hold on to familiar imagery just the same. Gifts we receive prove how popular we are; books signify knowledge; trophies or certificates are symbols of achievement. There is nothing wrong with a few well-placed memorabilia spreading comforting or encouraging vibes; it is about quantity. Kids rarely own 75 security blankets; they do not burden themselves with them or suffocate themselves underneath. How much stuff does it take to feel safe, to feel rich or secure? What does *enough* feel like? "The more stuff I stack around me, the more secure I am," is a misunderstanding. Belongings can do many things, but making us permanently feel safe and loved is outside their remit.

Security is never in stuff. It is found in having the confidence to handle any experience that life might throw our way. The storms will come, but we are steering our boat.

Create identity

We long for soul mates, for the community that understands where we are coming from and knows what we are all about. Identifying with a nation, region or religion meets the innate desire to belong; to be part of a greater good. By supporting a football team, worshipping a certain type of music, joining a party, parish or community, we move into the equivalent of an emotional home. As a fan we can live and express feelings of individuality and union at the same time. Granny collects tea pots; a colleague has amassed hundreds of vinyl records; friends are enthusiastic about apps, model airplanes or vintage cartoons. Stacks of ancient theatre programmes or school exercise books reassure us, "I did that – that's me." We pick and choose beliefs, clothes and shades of terracotta and perform a series of passionate identifications with artefacts; selecting them from the cultural market garden, hoping they will form a harmonious, thousand-petalled display that, the picture of our soul. Ultimately we are accumulating an essence. An art collection as an outlet for creativity; the movie compilation as the manifested desire to do some acting one day or a stint in comedy circles. Model planes symbolise speed, getting somewhere fast; aspirations of reaching goals, of freedom...

Go on a safari into your very own jungle of things. What image(s) are you attached to? Which essence are you hoarding? How could you get closer without having to put up one shelf after another? Endless rows of books might stand for (please delete as appropriate), "I'm well read / widely travelled / open minded / educated / eclectic / enlightened / cool / classy / different / intelligent / witty /

imaginative / spiritual / special / an art lover / lateral thinker / reformer / revolutionary / a good dad / in the know / committed to personal development and/or saving the planet..." What is the headline above your shelves, spelt out in invisible ink?

We want to be respected and loved and use objects to communicate this. "Look at this stuff, that's how unique I am! Please love me for what I'm wearing / driving / listening to..." Of course we know deep down that others do not like us for our collections of handbags or sophisticated living room interiors. If we make people laugh, we can do without the ultimate leather-bound twelve volume jokes collection. And if we have not been abundantly blessed with a sense of humour and/or the gift of the gab, even the most elaborate compilation will not be able to help change that. We communicate through our being, what we are outshines everything we hoard, say or do.

Cross-cultural living is a challenge because we have to keep more than one identity alive. One client said, "We live two lives, a contemporary Western and a traditional Indian one. I have to store the Christmas decorations as well as Saris and Dwali paraphernalia."

When thinking about status it gets interesting as soon as we start sidestepping beloved clichés like the red open-top sports car. Status symbols are chameleons and adopt the most varied of formats. They are tools to communicate an image and we all use them to broadcast our own personal messages. For some it is about brands, for others it is about avoiding them. They go to great lengths to only ever use local, organic or recycled goods in order to distance themselves from the shallow consumerism of a throwaway society. The big relief: trying to impress others never works anyway, so we might as well call it a day and stop sweating the small stuff.

We are not what we have, we are what we are. We are our story, a mosaic of experience puzzle pieces laid out in a magnificent, brilliantly unique pattern. How about expanding a collection that we started years ago? Key items might still be missing: a dream holiday, an encounter or a class that we always fancied having a go at. How about stockpiling memorable moments instead of things? The most intriguing compilation of all does not require dusting and we can even take it with us in the end – our collection of experiences.

Do the 'right' thing

Recipes are a mysterious phenomenon. They must be in the Top Ten of all time favourite hoards as it seems to be impossible to resist the urge to amass those randomly torn out pages and stacks of stained books. Collected even by those who dislike the idea of getting serious about chopping and do not know their pot from their pan. Recipes are symbols for committing to a way of life where wholesome home cooked meals are placed on tables featuring freshly cut flowers and happy people gathered around, laughing and singing. The exercise bike is another example of an aspirational item. It has been sitting there for ages, getting in the way and taking up a ridiculous amount of space. However, far more than merely a dust-collecting annoyance it is about our ambitions to keep fit; to dedicate ourselves to a healthy lifestyle and to do the right thing. We cannot bring ourselves to part with it because that would be the outward signal of giving up. Besides, we do not like getting things wrong or wasting anything as this would equal hurting the planet. (And praise for our good deeds, if you wouldn't mind!) We are special flowers; we prefer to bloom while someone else is watching. Speaking of flowers, one client emailed me:

> *"Here is a variation on the old ‚can't throw it away until it's completely worn out' predicament. I like gardening. I'm not particularly good at it but I like it. The problem is that I can never cut anything back or dig it up until the very last flower has died. This means that during the summer some plants take over and smother smaller plants because I can't bear to cut them back! Also, at the end of the year when you want to get ready for the winter – prune back, move things around, etc; I'm always too late to do it because the last flowers don't die until the frost gets them, by which time you can't cut back and move because things would die. This means that it never gets done. No more! Last Autumn I had a week off and everything got cut back, regardless. So I was able to get the garden organised and ready for winter. It's made such a difference. And this summer nothing is being allowed to outgrow its allotted space. Strange, I've never made the connection between all this and clutter hoarding, but it's definitely there."*[1]

Irreversible decisions, indeed any 'cut offs', are tricky as they feature a remote possibility of getting it wrong. There is no undo button for giving away unwanted presents and inherited china and we go to great lengths to avoid feeling guilty. At the end of a flight one of my clients took left-over airline bags with mini-toothpaste, socks and plastic cutlery because they would have been trashed otherwise. We burden ourselves with useless stuff because we

---

[1] Quotes in Italics mark feedback emails that I have received from clients over the years.

cannot bear the 'waste'. Right underneath the layers of dust are layers of guilt. "That was so expensive." Unfortunately that dreadful impulse buy is not reversed simply by hanging onto it. Why do we kid ourselves with DIY-definitions of what constitutes 'dear' instead of calling the true treasures precious and never stopping to count down lifespan reverentially in days?

Other gluey arguments: "I wanted to look into / do / finish that one day." When? "My grandmother wore this ring." We are not violating memories of late loved ones if we do not cling indefinitely to every item they left behind. Letting their things peacefully move on helps us do the same. A client stored her late mother's piano and electric organ in her tiny living room even though she never intended to play them. The room was so full of memories that the door no longer opened. She did not have access to the heart of her flat; years without friends sitting on the sofa because she could not bear the thought of "Throwing my mother away". Our loved ones do not expect us to bury ourselves with them out of grief and feelings of obligation. They want us to be happy.

In our part of the planet custom dictates purchasing, gift wrapping and handing over 'a little something' to express love and appreciation. Alas, the delight often ends as soon as the wrapping has come off. "*Oh no, please.*" We are trying to camouflage our disappointment and come up with a half-smile and arm movements that we hope might remotely resemble enthusiasm for the grim sweater or unspeakable vase that are off the radar on the planet of style we live on. However, a heartfelt "Thank you" does not make us a fake. We appreciate the effort, time and money invested by the giver because they were hoping to please us. If we manage to receive and retain *this* treasure in our heart, gratefully accepting the essence – love, symbolised in a gift – we can let the object move on. We can send it back out into the world, trusting that it will find a home where it is truly welcome. Most of us already own more stuff than we can delightfully integrate into our life which makes the infamous gift idea such a challenge. A client shared how her mum had asked her one day to only give her presents that she would want to get back. Ever since, they have been enjoying concerts together or eating out to celebrate birthdays and other occasions. Glorious events are handy gifts; they come without a use-by-date and do not take up storage space. Another bonus is that we are spared the worry of whether the individual already owns that gift-experience. A husband once asked his wife for a special Christmas gift: the promise to put an end to harking back; no more dishing up of past mistakes but the chance to start over with a clean slate. One client recalled, with tears in her eyes, how her husband had brought tea and toast to her bedside when she was unwell. She had been given diamond rings but this caring gesture was the gift that she treasured most. What truly priceless non-item presents could we shower friends and family with?

One of the most popular excuses to cling to something unused goes like this, "I've got this precious XYZ and don't want to *waste* it. I can only give it away to a good new home." (We are not talking pets here, we are talking stuff.) The generous giver would not mind a written guarantee certificate either, stating how potential recipients had a proven (preferably dire) need for the gift, qualified as 110% worthy and would be forever grateful.

Are we worthy owners? Is the item in good hands while having to stay with us? The most tragic waste of all is to banish an object into some gloomy storage space where it is condemned to gather dust, unused and heartbroken. Imagine how ecstatic someone else would be with it. How they would adore wearing it; revere reading it; be wild about listening to it. Only our insistence on not 'wasting' prevents this passionate love affair between our surplus item and its new owner; while we remain self-righteously immune to the irony of it all. Our trash could be someone else's treasure! Take the musical instrument that has forever fallen silent (no, the grandchildren – who have yet to be born – won't want it in 35 years time either, so let's forget about that way out). The guitar could carry on singing and dancing through a room with someone else. Possibly even live to see a stage!

So do yourself a favour and declutter the most ridiculous of excuses, "I don't know who to give it to." Where there is a will there is a way. The day after the clearout a leaflet drops through the door, our favourite charity announces a collection. Asking around or googling will bring up infinite charitable shops, organisations and good causes that are happy to unburden us: fundraising raffles at a local school or playgroup, children's home or shelter. As members of www.uk.freecycle.org, we can send one email and someone will collect even our bulky or electrical items.

Why not put some books we are no longer desperate to own into a shoe box and stick a sign on which announces at the next party: "Take us home if you like." Guests are leaving with a smile, "I came with one present and am leaving with two, thank you." Such spontaneous bringers of joy love lounging in communal areas of apartment blocks to delight the neighbours. Pieces of furniture have been known to venture out into the road to fearlessly embark on a new life of purpose. The unwanted chair is sitting on the drive, proudly showing off the handwritten message that propels it towards new adventures 'Please take me away!' And sure enough, a few hours later it has hitched a lift. Even pots and plants are joining in on the move. We refused to admit it to ourselves, but we were getting slightly exasperated with their 'having-grown-too-big-ness'. So we stopped dusting or repotting them and at some point in our passive-aggressive resentment we even started to 'forget' watering them, feeling terribly guilty. We never intended to kill them off; we just could not cope with that rubber plant any longer. Offered to passersby it now makes someone else's life complete. The only thing missing in their brand new flat was an oversized foliage plant. We are free as a bird and the new owners will inundate our ex with all the water and love it could wish for. We all live happily ever after.

In times when goods are plenty, the habit of 'waste not' becomes a burden. While allegedly worrying about 'squandering' coffee-table books or designer jackets, we try to float away from responsibility on an unfit raft made of cardboard and leather. Occupying ourselves with clutter-shifting-DIY brings welcome distraction from more serious waste: that of lifetime. How disheartening for the brand new day if all we use it for is to get through it, somehow, just about. Time does not want to be killed. The most heartbreaking waste lies beyond the world of objects, in frittering away another month, making ourselves at home in the weeks as if the next dawn was guaranteed forever. How about no longer pouring down the drain those potential joys we could experience but do not allow ourselves to? Apparently one of the most common regrets is "I wish that I had let myself be happier."

What we do does not matter all that much; it is about how we go through our day. How do we want to unwrap this one-of-a-kind morning? No more overlooking the misty magic of white fog clinging to treetops. Noticing how the wind is playing catch with leaves. Joining in, humming along to the gorgeously bright sparkling Song of Now.

Act out inner rebellion

Anyone who grew up with tidying as a punishment might end up equating mess with freedom. Contrary to art studio clichés however, creativity does not thrive in permanent chaos. After the brilliant idea has been born it has to rely on its down-to-earth cousins, discipline and organisation to stay alive, to manifest successfully and to turn into visible genius.

Our parents might have passed away a long time ago, but we are still sitting in our bedroom (that has turned into a flat by now), triumphantly defiant "I am *not* tidying up!" We can scatter stuff wherever we like; this is our place after all. We employ mess to get our own back and have gone to the barricades as some sort of time warped opposition against carers who used to invade our room to 'tidy up'. As in, dared to mess around with our things and therefore with us, violating both our sanctuary and our privacy.

A bit of a mess can also come in handy to demonstrate to those who live with us that they never help out. Without our saintly efforts, chaos would take over in no time. Perhaps we feel left alone with the responsibilities we are burdened with, that nobody seems to take off our shoulders or at least helps us carry. While living together we feel all alone.

Alternatively, disorganisation can be a means to keep people away. Perhaps we shared a home with flatmates or a partner before, but somehow stuff got in the way. Single's homes often have literally no space left for a potential companion and their belongings. Couples who remary later in life often end up staying in their respective homes as they cannot bring themselves to let go of their surroundings in order to move on and move in together.

Clutter as an outward SOS of pain inside can result from having to hang our hat on a lone perch. One client who lived by herself said, "When my sister shouts at me because of the mess, I feel as if at least someone cares."

In the short term we might delight in this 'rebellion', but sooner or later it becomes tainted by the fact that we no longer enjoy residing among piles. We dream of entertaining once we have sorted the place out. We might even go to the lengths of avoiding our home, putting in extra long hours at the office, filling the diary to the brim, stopping by for bed and breakfast and off again.

At work we create sophisticated paper sculptures on the desk to demonstrate to ourselves, our colleagues and the world at large just *how* busy we are. Paper pile lighthouses send out blinking signals: we would not mind the odd word of acknowledgement for our efforts, praise even, every now and again. Unfortunately the message gets lost in translation and others misinterpret our dishevelled desk space as lack of efficiency or expertise.

Organising is not about waving goodbye to spontaneity and funky fun and sticking colour coordinated labels on everything that cannot run away fast enough. It is about keeping the chaos that so relentlessly tries to invade our life at bay. Staying on top of our agenda means that we can afford time to recharge and award ourselves much needed breaks from chores that raise their ugly heads as soon as we try to sit down for a cuppa. Life does not have to consist of the same old, same old day after day. A mini-clearout is like an upgrade from mere functioning; we get to fly through the day feeling truly alive, marvelling at those wonders we call clouds and creepy crawlies. If we stay in control of our diary, we create space for the unexpected and discover opportunities for growth in between the chores, even *in* the chores.

Everybody deserves an inspiring living and working environment. Being organised does not give us a life sentence as the nerdy fusspot or tedious bore, stuck in repetitive habits, forever straightening checkered table cloths and brushing off invisible crumbs. Organising works without doilies and net curtains, without ceilings caving in on daily vacuumed shag pile rugs.

Getting rid of a mess is uplifting because, excuse the pun, being in messes depresses. Getting our act together and tying up loose ends brings clarity to our homes and our lives. Once we stop running away and face our clutter we can create a home that fills us with strength and joy, where every coming home is a home coming. Where we can bake soul pancakes, rest, relax and get the odd holiday vibe just from boarding the sofa. Where we can take off or come down as we wish, redirecting the energy of our rebelliousness to causes far more worthy than clutter.

Welcome to outer space!

Keep options open

The camping experience can be conveniently recreated at home, without a stove or air mattress in sight. Stopping short of pitching a tent, a house can look as if the campers have just moved in or are about to move out, even though the dwellers have lived at this address for years.

Light bulbs are dangling from the ceiling just until suitable lamp shades have been located. Curtains and blinds are still waiting for their turn to be ticked off the to-do-list. 'Home-campers' never make a home for themselves and they are not sure why. It might be the dim feeling that they do not deserve a more charming environment or the subliminal fear that making themselves at home would be equal to getting stuck permanently in this apartment, city or relationship. For the time being, until a perfect solution has been found, they make do. And suddenly another two years have disappeared into thin air.

Sometimes we avoid committing ourselves for fear of missing out on something better. Settling on one residence implies rejecting others. If we keep sitting on the fence, the 'Happy Ending' might ring the doorbell tomorrow. One client resented her apartment for not being situated in the beloved French Provence, but in a particularly uneventful town in Britain. Even if we approve of the where, we might resist the how. The current abode is not the longed for mortgaged property but 'only' a rented one; ground floor instead of penthouse; no garden; garden too small, too large, too green, not green enough, too overlooked and not south-west facing. 'Home-campers' know deep down that they will not stay forever, so why bother. The apartment block might be due a major overhaul at some point, or the neighbours do not live up to expectations. There are worries about catchment areas or commuting or some other concern we can make up as we bumble along through life. Campers refuse to tie themselves down. Maybe they have had to follow a job or a partner but would rather be settled somewhere else, thank you very much. They feel a need to keep their options open.

Here is the bad news: as long as we refuse to make ourselves at home in our own home; as long as we do not drop anchor, at least temporarily; we *will* stay stuck. We need foundations in order to move on; the future refuses to be built on wobbly makeshift arrangements.

"I moved into my flat ten years ago and was convinced that I wouldn't be there long as I was ultimately looking to move into a house. I never purchased proper storage such as extra shelves or cupboards, most of my belongings lived in large plastic boxes and I didn't worry about decorating or changing anything. As I wasn't getting anywhere in looking for a house I made the decision to make some small changes in the flat. I didn't tackle the storage issue but after several years of making do, I bought blinds for every room and also painted my bedroom rather than thinking that I wouldn't be here long so it wasn't worth it. I got to the stage where I was content to stay in the flat indefinitely. And then a few weeks ago, I went along to a new development nearby and I have fallen in love with the building plans for a house which I think would suit my needs perfectly!"

We start to build a rewarding relationship with our home as soon as we focus on its positive features. Thanks to whichever pad we happen to be staying in at the moment, the rain hits a roof instead of our head when we are asleep. Doors open for us and shut behind us; we enjoy shelter, security and privacy.

If the idea of a home as your castle makes you want to run, skip the garden gnome option. We do not have to settle down into dreaded mid-sized mid-town back garden cosiness; suffocating in daffodils, stuck in stuckness. Beauty refuses to be squeezed into one-size-fits-all. It keeps our soul alive, no matter what shape it takes. As soon as we have created our own unique version of beauty and truly arrived in our home, we are ready to set off towards the next milestone.

III Clearing as an art of living

The chances are that by now you are no longer looking at clearing as some fifth-rate option to while away twenty minutes of torrential rain. You have caught the clearing bug and you cannot keep your enthusiasm to yourself, telling everyone and their dog about the epiphany that is the decluttering of the sock drawer. You have just bumped into a friend and he is listening patiently, nodding in agreement (as he cannot get a word in edgeways anyway) while you go on. And on. "It's the most exhilarating excitement, honestly. Hard to believe for the uninitiated, I know, but it *is* personal development in action!" Your friend has finally managed to make up an excuse to say goodbye and rushes off. As soon as he arrives home, he has a go at the sock drawer.

Clearing is contagious and reintroduces joy as a core subject on the syllabus of the everyday. Welcome to lesson one, rookie and advanced alike: how do I live light-hearted and free, with smiles readily tap dancing from my lips? The art of decluttering might look a bit, well, 'stuff-y' at first but you could not ask for more profound concepts crammed together in one storage box of tricks – ready to unfold at the first timid decluttering attempts. Clearing class features some of the most fascinating topics in personal growth. Here is a taster of what the glamorous syllabus has in store: letting go, making decisions, developing intuition, managing energy levels... You do not have to sit a single exam but are still awarded a 'finals' certificate. Not a mere piece of paper of course, instead a masters degree in the art of living life to the full. No more vague waiting around for the tomorrow that never comes, no more tentative tiptoeing through yet another year; rather jumping out of bed in the morning, ready to dive into whatever lies ahead.

Bye bye prejudice

Belongings make us belong. First of all to the place where we keep most of them and have some on show; shifting things about, eternally 'home-staging'. If we nose around as a pretend stranger in our own home, what can we find out about the person(s) living here? If the place spells out overload, we might have buried ourselves under stuff. The outside mirrors the inside, clutter has protective qualities and walls are erected for a reason. So let's not squander even the tiniest amount of precious energy on self-criticism. This padded, sheltering environment was what we have needed to date and was therefore exactly right. We break free and let go of our lovely little habit of constantly judging everything, including ourselves, unfavourably. *"The most valuable thing I took away from the class was to stop ‚berating' or ‚beating myself up.' Over and over this morning I have successfully intercepted my thoughts!"*

The time has come and the end is near for taking cover behind protective barriers, which is now declared yesterday's habit. We start to dig ourselves out, bag after bag towards the dazzlingly light and airy feeling of The New. Granting a generous amnesty for all baddies involved: boxes, bags and their owners. We have stopped judging ourselves for being a bit of a collector and extend this relaxing attitude to those around us. In the clearing world judging does not get condemned from a 'one has to be good at all times'-angle, it is just that wagging of index fingers at the world at large happens to be a first class waste of energy. As long as we consider ourselves superior to someone, we will keep feeling inferior in other instances. As a rule, judgments say more about us than the assessed party. We slot ourselves neatly into categories with rigid views on styles or 'proper' ways of doing things: conservative, alternative, traditional, progressive – been there, got the label. 'Normal' is just a setting on the dryer.

Entering and leaving the global stage we are all the same, on a soul level any judgement remains prejudice. We have to make do with superficial assessments, will never know where another soul is headed or what their journey is all about. We are dancing together through space and time as snowflakes, none like the other. Here one moment, melted away the next. Dwellers of the lands beyond measuring scales, the only feature we share is our uniqueness.

"This lady seems to be getting rounder by the day." Actually, this lady is getting more pregnant every day. Why invest time and energy into judging if we are going to reverse our judgement sooner or later? Intriguing interior design choices of our fellow beings make a good starting point to practice our novel attitude of nothing but equanimity. Different snowflakes choose different paraphernalia; deer antlers might induce shudders of wellbeing in some and make others want to run away. Some people think driving on the left is the right way to do it. Anything goes.

There we are, convinced we have found the truth and nothing but the truth, only to conclude a few years further along the timeline that the exact opposite must be the epitome of wisdom. A parable illustrates this in a story about a man and his horse. One day the horse ran away. The neighbours were sorry about the man's misfortune. The man said, "It might be a misfortune, it might not. Who knows?" Then the horse came back with a wild horse in tow, making the man proud owner of two horses and the neighbours happy about his stroke of luck. The man said, "It might be, it might not, who knows?" His son was badly hurt while breaking the wild horse in. The neighbours were sorry. "Who knows," said the man. Recruits came to the village, drafting all young men but the severely injured one. "How lucky!" the neighbours exclaimed…

Energy stuck in judgement is missing elsewhere. We can access it by chucking out the permanently broken scales at the next clearout.

Eyes are the lens, thoughts the camera, the picture we see is 'reality'. There are as many realities as there are human beings. All of us navigate with two unique maps over our little blue planet, one being a map of 'the way things are', our personal version of reality. The second one is a map of 'how things should be', or values. We filter everything through these templates, which makes reality an interpretation.

A traveler talks to an old lady who is sitting outside her house, enjoying the evening sun and smiling at passersby. "I'm thinking about settling in this town. What are the people like around here?" asks the traveler. The lady replies, "What are they like where you live now?" The traveler says, "Well, that's why I want to get away. I can't stand anybody there. They are very selfish people and only look after themselves." The lady replies, "You will find the people in this town to be the same." Not long afterwards another man passes by and stops to sit down for a little chat. "I'm thinking of moving and have considered this place as one of my options. What is it like to live here?" The lady asks him, "What is it like where you come from?" He replies, "Oh the people in my town are wonderful. We look out for each other and help one another where we can." The lady says, "You will find the people in this town to be the same."

Perception is reality. We can unlock undreamt of energy resources as soon as we stop wanting to be right. Choosing our battles wisely we let others decide on seating arrangements, colour schemes and timeframes. When it comes to inner priorities, we do not give an inch and dig our heels in for the right to stay alive on the inside: embark on a trip, class, retreat or have half hour of time out in our favourite cafe.

If less energy leaks out into power struggles or inner resistance, more is available for sustained sowing and reaping.

Letting go without regret

Nothing remains the same, even if we are doing our bit to stop the clock and join Ye goode olde days Club. "The youth of today loves luxury. They have bad manners, contempt for authority, show disrespect for elders and love chatter in place of exercise. Children are now tyrants, they contradict their parents, cross their legs and tyrannise their teachers." Socrates made those observations some 2500 years ago and his view has found supporters ever since. While we are still grumbling, this impossible next generation goes ahead and comes up with the next incomprehensible gadget, the sole purpose of which is to do our head in: the wheel, the steam engine, the smart phone app... It is hard to keep up, the world out there seems to be whizzing about ever faster, spinning off profound change roughly every twenty seconds. "I prefer a pace on the saner side of slow", you might say now. "I don't want too many changes too fast." So we leave our home interiors untouched and refuse to run with the latest makeover schemes, the unchanging wall-paper pattern a fortress against the vicissitudes of life. We boycott DIY fads, go to bed and wake up again in a homemade illusion of permanence. We do our best to resist, but change could not care less about our defiance and carries on changing, doing what it does best: being inevitable. In nature nothing stays the same, stagnation equals death. Our body replaces millions of cells per second, every seven years we get to live in a completely rebuilt model. Biological and economic systems break down when there is no flow; holding on sooner or later blocks and destabilises any structure or organism. Small clearing successes are tentative steps towards getting in sync with the universal process of 'out with the old, in with the new'. We can regulate our speed, go up a gear or slow down again, gradually getting used to dealing with grief, our natural reaction to any change. As soon as we start sorting, memories come rushing in. When bidding farewell to a present of someone who is no longer a part of our life, we practice coping with loss and the fear of being abandoned. We get to have a trial run at saying goodbye forever feels like; a skill that will be called for when beloved people, animals or circumstances leave our life. Once we know what we are grieving about when we let go of an object, any old clearout transforms into a free therapy session. Clutter turns into Doctor MakeYouWell and assists with a life-affirming renewal of self. "Does this object inspire me; does it bring me closer to myself? Does it imbue me with courage and joy and make me come alive?"

There are always ongoing road works on the way forward; areas where we could do with pointers in the right direction, or at least less diversions. Work might not go entirely according to plan or our personal life may not live up to expectations. We could do with a bit more money, more time or new faces in our circle of friends. We are not asking a lot from life, all we want is to live happily ever after. Clearing is an opportunity to face the process of constant change, welling up at the sight of baby shoes or children's' drawings. Handling the belongings of a late loved one tugs at our heartstrings and mirrors the transitory state of our being. Letting go of those reminders can be so challenging that we resort to shifting and parking them in the loft. What we resist persists. Refusing change is a considerable energy expense that cannot halt the eternal process of metamorphosis. There is no past tense to today; there is no future in the immediate now. This cosmically patched together quilt of moments and minutes is the only life we will ever have. Change means development, going forward; transience and growth go together. Nothing is ever lost, it just changes form and a change of form is never destructive. Life is becoming, and death is part of this process. When a loved one has passed away, we have to *handle* the memories they leave behind; take them up one by one and deal with them. If there is only enough strength to leave everything untouched we need to give ourselves more time.

Often we do not want to part with an object because we are afraid to lose access to a related memory. A group photograph of memorabilia can make it easier to let those reminders move on. We are able to let go of objects once we feel it as a truth that we can never lose their essence because we carry it in us. Experiences we have gained through dealing with an object have contributed towards who we are today. Even as the symbol leaves our life, this cannot be undone.

Children outgrow their clothes and toys and so do we. Now that we are proficient at decommissioning objects, we discharge dated thinking patterns that somehow got away with hibernating unnoticed in the back of our mind. Next in line for a clearout: antique acquaintances, ill-fitting habits or ways of reacting. We decide to get real and weed through plans which, let's face it, this lifetime will not be sufficient to bring to fruition.

"I'm on a roll, yet again, getting rid of all those projects that I will never get around to. Like the books I never read, these projects sit in the corner of my office and I move them from pillar to post until, now, they are going out the front door."

Festive occasions are institutionalised opportunities to express appreciation and love. It is entirely up to us which of the expectations on offer we want to subject ourselves to. If they cause stress, out they go. Often we put ourselves under pressure by setting standards for ourselves we would not expect from anyone else.

The idea of ownership seems to be some sort of weird misunderstanding. Native American Indians refused to subscribe to a concept where the land they held sacred would 'belong' to someone by marking a few lines on a piece of paper. We arrive on this planet without material possessions and we cannot take any with us when we leave. This makes us temporary custodians for generations to come. In the art of letting go we practice living change in a constructive way and treat ourselves to a generous helping of equanimity; one of its most pleasant side effects.

The clearing recipe for a fulfilled life is to learn from an experience and then move on. Collect brand new ones year after year instead of repeating the same dozen for decades.

We can only reach out for one another or embrace the new with hands that are empty.

Make those decisions

Doing the living thing can be exhausting. Making decisions day in, day out eats up energy; so we put the kettle on, leave things as they are and place that piece of paper here for now. Long-term this non-strategy muddles things up and prevents freedom from fighting its way through to the sofa. Freedom is tiring. Permanently having to ask, "Do I still want this?" gets on our nerves and teaches us an essential life skill: how to make decisions proactively. Self-storage is a booming industry because we volunteer to pay for accommodation for our material ex-flatmates, incurring fines on a monthly basis for postponing the showdown with our stuff. Seasonal items, sports or camping gear require storing; anything else means we are dipping our toes into the treacherous waters of avoidance tactics. Think of the spaghetti. We stay responsible wherever on the globe we stash our clutter. *Getting ourselves together* means exactly that: gather scattered belongings from assorted countries, parents' lofts and friends' houses, face up to what is ours and deal with it.

Clearing exercises the decision-making muscle. Bit by bit, we learn to trust that bad decisions make great stories and that there are no wrong turns; only diverse ways of doing things. Research and development teams run thousands of trials until a breakthrough is achieved. Every experience is a success. There is no failure, just feedback.

There is only one seriously bad decision and that is to refrain from decision making altogether because this will revert us back into the default mode of making do. It is a slippery slope indeed from the heights of steering our fate towards mere reacting and getting by, where suddenly another two years have trickled down the hourglass and none of our hazy hopes have come true. We outsource whole areas of our life and hand over responsibility to so called experts. (Ever wondered what 'perts' are and what turns them into ex-perts? Anyway we digress.) Following the advice of experts is advantageous in that we have got someone to blame should things not work out. Coming to our own conclusions is a comparatively rocky road that is paved with longwinded research, trial and error. Who has the time? So to overstate our case here: doctors, pharmacists, physiotherapists and nutritionists are in charge of physical health, analysts and spiritual guides look after the rest. Following guidelines and sticking to recommended doses frees us from having to arrive at our own conclusions. How many files bulging with bank statements or telephone bills 'should one have?' Just like real life, organising does not come with a one-size-fits-all, 'this is how you do it' patent remedy. We are the experts who can figure out what feels too much, too little or exactly right. Collector, connoisseur or minimalist – what role suits best? How many books or shoes can be joyfully integrated into the everyday? It might be five for us and five hundred for someone else. It is very freeing to stay in charge of our decisions and rely on our own authority.

Decluttering as a runway towards self-determination – ready for takeoff? Come aboard.

Take responsibility

"There's never enough time," is such a lovely excuse – which is probably why we tend to overuse it, occasionally. It is an excuse though. The thing about time is, if we look hard enough, we might find some, somewhere. We might even make some. Where did we get it from, oodles of it, traipsing around the shops, attending charity auctions or filling shopping baskets online to then patiently await the umpteenth delivery? It may come as a surprise, but we have created our environment in its present shape and form. Interior design might not be the term that sums up our approach, which was overall closer to burying our head in the sand and ignoring the mail and the arrival of a few of those 'buy one get three free' bargains too many. Now that they have got hold of a residents' parking space in our home we are too polite or too weary to kick them out. Even though we are more than fed up with playing hide and seek, a game they cannot get enough of.

Seneca noticed some 2000 years ago that it is not a problem of a shortage of time, but rather about too much time not being used. Option number one is to list all the reasons why it is impossible right now to regain control over paperwork, kitchen cabinets and life in general. Option two is to switch off various screens earlier than usual; tear ourselves away from social and less social media; get up twenty minutes earlier or cut down on worrying time by combining it with a micro-clearout and test-scribble through a box of pens. The odd five minutes here and there add up to impressive chunks of time, over time. Clearing is an invitation to live up to our life. Own it, warts and all.

Blaming, even our charming friend 'lack of time', comes with obvious advantages but also has a major downside: it disempowers. If we want to stay in charge of our things and our life we have to take the initiative and right now would be a good time to get started. We have to make arrangements to leave our niece the ring that she always admired before the decision will be taken out of our hands. Why burden our descendants with clutter when they are struggling with grief? Let's get ticking and eat the frogs first: meet the financial advisor, draw up that will.

Getting away from excuses is a powerful accelerator that blows up clutter chains with a double dose of dynamite made of honesty and accountability. Free at last.

Appreciate our unique journey

We just clutter-busted a stack of stuff – no elaborate rearranging, no decisionless reshifting, no dodgy goings on – everything got sorted. Tick! Wow! The high lasts a full 25 seconds, and then they are here, sneering. "Those bits of paper, big deal. You must be having a laugh – loft, spare room and garage are still untouched! If you keep sorting at that pace you've got your work cut out darling, you'll be at it for another 15 years, minimum." The inner critics are determined to hang around for good and they are never impressed, no matter how heroic our achievements. They know where they can hit us hardest and they do: "You are a mess!" Rule Number One: *Do not listen!!* Shush them out of your mind, turn the key in the lock and put a bunch of flowers bang in the middle of the freed up space. Enjoy how promising this reclaimed area feels, a blank canvas to be filled with future delights. Something wonderful has been achieved and now, for a change, we notice it every time. Great views courtesy of the just cleaned window; snuggling into crisp sheets; scribbling into the ideas book with a pencil sharpened to perfection. Other big deals: our email signature supports a charity in their good cause; someone will find a card in their letterbox tomorrow, just because. Tiny steps are the most important ingredients of successful energy management, they are powerful agents of change. Do not be fooled by ordinary standard measurements; the greatest achievements can look miniscule from the outside. A major breakthrough for one client was to let go of a tiny white medication dispenser. *"My mother-in-law had been living with us until she passed away. When I could finally bring myself to part with that symbol, I knew I was ready to let her go. It amazes me how decluttering on the level of objects also frees up your heart and your mind. I feel less confused and much more balanced."*

Why ignore progress just because it is not visible from the moon? It is easy to get stuck on what is not working; what we do not yet or no longer have; or to focus on what we have achieved. It is more difficult to concentrate on the step ahead if we keep distracting ourselves by glancing sideways to suss out what others are up to, as illustrated in the legend of Rabbi Sussyah. "In the coming world nobody will ask me, 'Why have you not been Eliah or Abraham?' I will be asked, 'Why have you not been Sussyah?'"

Clearing zooms us back in on celebrating our successes; personal milestones we have reached and passed. We take a step back to marvel at this performance of a lifetime: traumas we have overcome, relationships we have built, renewed or ended. How often did the rug get pulled from under our feet, our heart broken? How often did we get up, dust ourselves off and carry on? Our story is a thriller packed with magnificent learning experiences, the script of which we are crafting day by day. We have achieved so much simply by getting to where we are today and being who we are now. This calls for celebration: you are being awarded the Nobel Prize for the hero or heroine of the everyday and presented with a well deserved medal of honour for challenges overcome and inspirational living done! Sticking it straight into a drawer is not an option; put it around your neck and parade up and down, ideally in front of a mirror. Go on, take credit, just this once.

Clearing is an opportunity to divert our attention away from the enormity of what is still to do and to focus on celebrating what we have achieved. Every clearing success is a confidence boost. Instead of going on about how far we still have to go (yawn), we acknowledge how far we have come. Someone else might be a natural at what we are struggling with, but that does not devalue our journey. The only person we can try to be better than is the person we were yesterday. Personal growth is about excelling ourselves; eventually clearing another one of those internal hurdles, however many attempts it might take.

Energy management as self-management

As long as we are at loggerheads with ourselves we cannot give. When running on empty, we can only take from others on an energy level. Every encounter is an energy exchange, every chitchat has an impact, leaving us fired up, exhausted or somewhere in between. Some people are like jump leads, others drone on about minor mishaps, depleting our enthusiasm reservoirs to critical levels. Which vibes are we spreading; power point or bottomless pit? Are we sucking any love or encouragement coming our way into the black hole of, "Well it's nice of you to say that, but...", without a chance of replenishing the soul. Once we are no longer working full-time at our own emotional building sites, we access an inner well of joy and start to radiate energy. How refreshing it is, and how rare, to enjoy the company of someone who is happy with their life and their lot. Someone who is not in waiting mode, not broadcasting frustration vibes because they have glued themselves into a job or a relationship for fear there is nothing else. They never buried their fire under Too Much Stuff and created a life that allows for joy and therefore energy. They can withdraw inside, stare into the flames of an inner campfire that is blazing away in their heart, and warm up all over. They feel no need to recharge through nagging, criticising, controlling or blanking out others and do not permit others to do this to them.

Attention energises. There are various tactics to fine-tuning and getting hold of this precious raw material. All time favourites are either talking incessantly or not talking at all; putting on the *poor me* hat or staging another instalment of an *I am the champion* routine. We have been equipped with two ears and one mouth and the weighting in this design might not be entirely accidental.

Many of us were brought up to believe in self-sacrifice and over-responsibility for others as positive values; to mistake constant rushing around for proof of being important and needed. Such convictions can darken our days into a greyish mash. Martyrs think they have to put everybody else first and do not only drive themselves to exhaustion but also drain people around them. We can only make others happy if we are at home with that feeling, illustrated in the quiz question: how many burnt out light bulbs are required to illuminate a stadium? 'Emotional contagion' is the term science applies to the fact that moods spread. Brain research shows that it is not what we say or do, but what we are that leaves its mark on our environment. Our being rewires neural pathways, both ours and those of the people we share our life with. Let's spoil the kids with the best present ever and be parents who are happy and fulfilled in their own right. Being content inside is how balanced surroundings come about so the to-do-list now goes topsy-turvy and features looking after number one as the top priority. Doing things that fill us with joy is no longer filed under egotism, but regarded as an essential tool for successful energy management that benefits all. Partners, friends and colleagues will be overjoyed about our post-clutter 'New Me' now also post-moody and fabulously un-cranky.

When we talk about a lack of time the underlying meaning is often "I haven't got the energy to tackle that by myself." Clearing teaches us to be economical with the strength we have at our disposal and do what we can, no less no more. We keep it manageable using mini-clearouts, limited to 10 minutes or 10 objects until we feel ready to pull off more extensive projects which are energetically much trickier. Clearing teaches us to monitor our energy levels in a proactive way instead of remaining at the mercy of seemingly uncontrollable fluctuations. How could we streamline routines to create space for essential recharge, doodling and daydreaming? We no longer cram activities into every last hour because we feel guilty if we are not bursting with being busy and justifying our existence by doing some-thing. We are human beings, not human doings. In running around mode we audition for the guest part of headless chicken. Clearing can serve as a reminder to keep doing and being in balance. After a stint of organising we sit down to indulge in a stint of cloud-spotting. Rest periods give the body a chance to carry out essential repair and rebuilding works. While relaxing in the tub we witness floating bubble continents collide to slowly blur into each other. Only when we have slowed down, chirrups do not just hit our eardrums but get through to us. Suddenly we hear the birds and see the light. We turn our head towards the stray that made it through the grey somehow, that sunray coming out of nowhere to caress our face.

The art of accepting

How often we brush aside a compliment or feel obliged to return it indicates how versed we are in the fine art of receiving graciously. We might be suffering from the 'inability-to-accept-syndrome', pushing back something good as soon as it tries to come our way, "Oh you shouldn't have!" Receiving can be more of a challenge than adopting the role of the giver where we get to feel generous and in control. When we have to accept, we might worry about having to return the favour or about creating expectations or even – eek – ending up owing. "You shouldn't have spent that much," is not exactly what the person who presents us with the most gorgeous bunch of peonies was hoping to hear. Kneejerk rejections devalue both the giver and the act of giving. Giving is such fun though, it lights a lantern in our heart. We love to do it and keep getting things for children because we cannot wait to see them jumping with joy, eyes lighting up. We look forward to their excitement and want to forget that this gift too will soon go under in the 'Floods of the Unused'. When we treat ourselves to the life-affirming pleasure of treating someone, we might get lucky and come across one of those rare creatures, the truly delighted, 'Oh how wonderful than you so much!'"recipient. Could that be you?

Any three year old is brilliant at accepting. It is peanuts to someone who can fly to Mars in a cardboard rocket and put their shoes on all by themselves. Ok, so the latter might not have worked out so far, but they are determined to have another go at it, shoving the carer aside with unrelenting optimism, "I can do it by myself!!" Only to be immediately followed by, "Can you help me?" There is no contradiction in a child's world between tackling something with all your might and asking for assistance should it not work out. Keeping this natural wisdom of 'hire up' alive seems to be one of the trickiest accomplishments while growing up. Requesting help requires courage and self-confidence which is why the 'I have to do everything by myself' complex is as widespread. Turning to some-one who knows more and is therefore more powerful in that interaction is a skill in itself. "I was never scared by what I didn't know," is how a business woman described the secret of her success. The cost of standing still can be higher than the cost of moving on. Where does that "I'm-alright-thanks," come from when some-one is trying to be of assistance? Why reject a helping hand, exclude opportunities, miss out on an experience or encounter?

We would still be sitting in caves and chewing on raw bones if the *thanks but no thanks* mantra had served as humanity's guiding principle so far.

Perfectionism is a killjoy and has been ousted from office. Now that we no longer have to get it right all the time, we can treat ourselves to a chaos drawer per room: open, chuck in with gusto, close. Brilliant. Being perfect is a stifling state of affairs; it suffocates growth which is all about becoming. Life is a constant exchange; the orchestra of the everyday does not feature soloists. Others produce pizzas and pyjamas for us, taught us how to read and write and a few other things along the way. They look after the water supply so we get to have our showers and cups of tea. They built the trains and planes that take us places and make sure that the light comes on when we turn the switch. Of course, we still insist on taking the lead in the comedy act, "Why do I always have to do *everything* by myself around here?" Most likely when something has gone wrong, just one of those little nothings that others would sort out in no time, as we keep telling ourselves. Just thinking about that flat tyre is too much: the dreaded little 'puff' sound still ringing in our ears, we are left with the joys of procrastination. "Tomorrow I'll fix that. At the weekend, latest." Both the easiest and the most difficult way out is to ask for help. Facing the cruel truth head on that we are actually not brilliant at doing everything. Assistance is lurking at every street corner, lying in wait to jump on us with a smile, "Can I help you?" Delegating is an option. Unbeknownst to us, amidst billions of fellow creatures there are people walking this planet who actually enjoy fixing tyres. Do we happen to be friends with one of them? If not, this is where the professionals come in, patiently waiting in their specialist shops to get us out of a jam because it is what they do for a living. We have to show up though, cut the homemade drama short, chuck the offending wheel in the boot and drive off to the repair shop. Leave the casualty with them, walk out, have a coffee with sunrays on the side. Come back, smiling. Let the pros know that they have saved our life, yet again. Thank them profusely, walk out smiling. Win win.

Life has things in store we could do without – grief, pain, death – and does not come with a 'no trauma for me please' option. We can allow pain to become all consuming and make us bitter; go numb and close down to prevent further agony from getting through. Or go through the motions, get drilled, ground and cut up as a diamond that is sparkling back out into the world what it had to go through. Inspired to ask new questions in new ways, search for answers in unchartered territory and redefine priorities. The deeper the furrows of pain are ploughed into a heart, the more joy it can hold. If we cannot get out of a place of distress, we can brave this tricky business of accepting assistance, even if it originates from unfamiliar regions of our universe. Acupuncture, NLP, reflexology, hands on/quantum/distance healing, coaching, crystals, Tai chi, Yoga, homeopathy, massage, reiki, astrology, Bachflower remedies, shiatsu, self-help, mudras, physiotherapy, osteopathy – the list is endless. Why not tuck in and munch our way up and down the menu until we come across our favourite healing dish. Mix, match and make up our own recipes.

"Learning is remembering," said Plato. The best teachers help us to access knowledge that is already inside of us. Following our intuition makes sense when we choose advisors. „Do I like the person behind the instructor / therapist / expert shop window? Is the life they lead inspiring to me?"

We can ask others for directions, but we have to do the walking. At birth we were given the pen to write our life story. Every day is a sentence, a month makes up a paragraph, every year opens a new chapter. Pages are being filled even if we do not get up to much. It is said that we will read our story in the end. Are you looking forward to a page-turner?

Refurbish relationships

The art of letting be

Another aspect that makes objects so entertaining is the fact that they are hardwired into relationships. The most frequently asked question at any clutter clearing event? "My partner / friend / daughter / parents have way too much stuff. What can I do about it?" Well, the short and the long of it is: nothing. Leave them be and start blitzing your stuff. There might be an incey wincey clearing project hiding away in our own home somewhere, waiting to be tracked down. As this is not a terribly appealing option we submit to temptation one last time and educate family members, friends or colleagues in need of our counsel. Except they are not. An easy way to spot if someone is after our input are clues in the form of questions like, "What do *you* think?" When asked, offer a 'best of my groundbreaking ideas' then let go and let be. We feel amazing once we let the rest of the universe get on with it.

Unsolicited subtle, or not so subtle hints, come with a Big Fat Pro: making others into a project takes the mind of our own issues and non-actions. Unfortunately there is also a Capital Con: nagging never works. Fault-finding is energetically a bad investment and has never shifted anybody closer towards any lights at the end of tunnels. Grass does not grow quicker if it is being pulled or pushed ever so gently and the same goes for human seedlings. Clearing can teach us to recognise the abuse in trying to force something or someone who is not ready, including ourselves. The magic formula is to change *our* reaction to an issue or a recurring situation.

One of the most important rules to bear in mind when clearing is to never trespass into throwing out what is not ours. How would we know what still holds practical or emotional value for someone else? He easily identifies her handbag collection as clutter, whereas she never got her head around what he needed all those wires for. Cluttered space is holy ground to the creator. If we come stampeding in with subtle accusations like, "What do you still need that rubbish for?!" the other party will retaliate, feeling hurt and misunderstood. What we have chosen becomes part of our sense of who we are. Sort things out together or double check with the owners, even if they are children. The only foolproof method to get others going is to start with yours truly and trust the clearing vibes to spread. They will do, fast and furiously, the positive energy that we generate jumpstarts people around us. The phone rings just after we have completed an organising project, Dad is bursting with pride. "You'll never guess what I've been up to! Here's a clue: I've been meaning to do this for ages – I finally cleared out the shed."

Although few things are harder to put up with than a good example, we do learn through resonance in our energy field. As soon as someone close can feel that we have turned the spotlight away from our pet project of 'helping them grow' and are concentrating on ourselves instead, they will make a contribution. Clearing is like a Mexican wave.

> *"It is true that our own actions get others going. I'm amazed about the change in my husband. He never let go of anything and was an absolute hoarder, but now that I have started to tackle*

my stuff the miracle has happened and he's having clearouts all of a sudden – without any prompting from my side!"

Arguments springing up about belongings taking up too much room or spreading all over the place mirror an imbalance in the relationship. One partner might even talk about *your* instead of *our* home. Make the interior a joint project. Are all residents represented in equal measures? Is the relationship visibly alive in its current form or are there medleys hanging around that remind of all sorts of exes: past life stages, by-gone relationships? Reaching a compromise on the level of objects is far more than symbolic and has a profound impact on relationships. Rebalancing the distribution of things is a powerful way towards readjusting the bigger picture. As a clutter clearing class participant reported: *"The most wonderful thing that has happened since I embarked on this journey of becoming lighter is that I have become friends with my family again."* When we get things done as a team we end power struggles and bring relationships into an equilibrium. And if we are currently looking for a partner, would we be able to fit them in? Is there room for someone in our wardrobe, our diary and our life?

The outside mirrors the inside not only at the material level; the people surrounding us are not a coincidence either. If the partner hoards stuff, we might find it difficult to let go of something on the inside, get stuck on a disappointment or resentment and that is being reflected. Who excels at doing our head in? A sideways glance in the psychological mirror brings enlightening reflections and the possibility of release. "I'm ready to let go of the part in me that annoys me about you." Sometimes parents complain about children who refuse to part with a single one of their 250 soft toys although they have run out of storage space years ago. Going back to the mirror idea, when did Mum or Dad last say goodbye to a habit or changed a routine, what are they holding on to?

If we feel balanced, our mood is not dependent on what others are doing or not doing. When someone is having a bad day and happens to be taking it out on us we refuse to be baited because we know that random accusations are about the insecurities or uneven temper of the person having a go rather than with us. However, this liberating insight does not let us off entirely as every issue surfacing in a relationship mirrors a challenge that we have avoided to look at within ourselves. Our relationships can only be as healthy as we are. Sometimes partners are not truly connecting but live with each other's conditioning. Take discussions about money as a case in point. Whereas for one it may stand for security, for the other it is a means for growth and adventure. If underlying values are not out in the open, arguments result from failing to grasp what makes the other person tick. In case we get bored with the family-ar drama, we are spoilt for choice. Which format of study, class or therapy suits you, Sir? Madam? – Go into orbit around the sun and shine on.

Having accomplished mega feats like pepping up our relationships with the abstinence from nagging, we extend our vocabulary in the language of love and pick what has proved most challenging so far. Was it mission impossible to find the right words, was touching too touching? How about the gift of time: an evening together, all gadgets turned off. Have you ever tried an impromptu rendition of "I just call to say..." over the phone? An overdose of appreciation on all available channels: texting, emailing and saying out loud the things we love about someone. Other good deeds of the day could be not to bring up a controversial issue or do something we do not have to do without insisting on credit; surprising friends or family with an art installation made of treats or let them discover heart shaped sticky notes with lovely messages all over the place. Have fun dreaming up your personalised collection of gems and indulge hoarder instincts by adding to it as if there were no tomorrow.

Non-judgment and unconditional love are powerful transformers; our biggest weaknesses are also our greatest strengths. An elderly Chinese lady had two large pots to collect water, each hung on the ends of a pole which she carried across her neck. One of the pots was cracked while the other one was perfect and always delivered a full portion of water. At the end of the long walk from the stream to the house the cracked pot arrived only half full, despairing of its imperfection and miserable that it could only do half of what it had been made to do. After two years of what it perceived to be bitter failure, it finally spoke out. "I'm so ashamed of myself because this crack in my side causes water to leak out all the way back to your house." The old lady smiled. "Did you notice that there are flowers on your side of the path but not on the other pot's side? I have always known about your little flaw, so I planted seeds on your side and every day while we walk back, you water them. For two years I have been able to pick the most beautiful flowers to decorate the table. Without you being just the way you are, their beauty would not grace the house."

Each of us has unique flaws and it is exactly those cracks that we have that make our lives together so intriguingly rewarding.

Setting boundaries

You have been thinking about this business idea, short story or fundraising event. You would love to have a go at painting, take up running again, listen to live music more often or set up a charity. Goals are useless if we do not create the time and space to implement them. Joining the queue and putting ourselves last can be less of an effort than stepping out of line. Luckily we can fall back on a certain something to get to grips with this tricky issue of setting boundaries – you might have a hunch? Yes, spot on: clutter clearing is the race track towards unheard of powers of self-assertion! Challenges approach under cover, another well meaning offer from Mum who is trying to palm something off on us. "I've got this spare shelf / cushion / picture frame, would you like it?" Well, *no* – but then again we do not want to come across as rude or ungrateful and we did turn her down last time. There must be some space left somewhere, surely, so why not? As the years go by this random acceptance of things leaves us with precious little room to manoeuvre. We lose sight of the bigger picture in a maze of ramshackle collections and get hazy about where we are headed.

Clearing is going back to the roots of our very own preferences, one mug at a time. "How do I want to furnish my home, what do *I* like? How do *I* want to live?" We do not have to store other people's stuff just because we have more space or a big heart. End up encircled by dreadful ornaments because we cannot bear the thought of hurting auntie who passed away years ago. Training sessions are off to a flying start when we have managed the first 'no' and prevented another unwelcome object from moving in with us, all steely determination underneath the pleasant smile. No more worrying we might hurt someone, miss out on something, might not be enough or not good enough. Items that inspire us help us win back a feel for ourselves; they are the signposts towards this idiosyncratic mystery called 'me'. The ability to say no when we feel like it is one of the most liberating achievements in personal development. The next step is to decline errands or tasks if we cannot afford the time or simply do not feel like doing them. The tiny favour has to go and find someone else to ask. It is a shame though: "I love helping out wherever I can and being there for others 24/7." There we are, having invested all this precious time and effort into carefully crafting our DIY halo – and now we have to switch it off. Then again, we were always the only one who could make out this shining circle above our head. Others only noticed the self-installed led weights that were dragging our shoulders into a permanent slump while we bravely forced another smile. Ditch the defect halo, wave goodbye to keeping up appearances and after this clearout to end all clearouts dance back into line with other mere mortals. Life is much more thrilling once we have handed in our notice as an apprentice saint.

When we have blown the dust off dated self-portraits, we get to see glimpses of the latest edition of 'I': still loyal, ever helpful, a good daughter, sister, auntie and an absolute dear all round – just without the slightest hint of martyrdom. Clearing has taught us to meet our own needs and not call it selfish. Now that we have got rid of the halo there is space to fit antennas, gauging readily which potential action or non-action would add or sap energy. We have now officially stopped beating about the bush to say what we are after, loud and clear and ever so charmingly. Soon everyone will have caught on that we stopped collecting cats ages ago and that we adore lilies and pistachio chocolates and would never say no to a football ticket. And while we are at it, we have started asking for what we want and stopped saying, "I'm fine," no matter how we feel. We have got rid of our apologising habit for good and we are not sorry about it.

Self-determination is another trophy waiting for us after round 25 of the clearing game. Once we stop fiddling with everybody else's pursuit of happiness we get a grip on our own and step out onto the sun deck, Chinese lanterns ablaze, nose in the breeze, jogging along towards a colourful horizon and a home where every room reflects the activities that are taking place there. Bedroom is another word for rest and relaxation, sleeping in a storeroom/larder/utility area is not quite as refreshing. If parts of the living areas double as a home office, a folding desk makes the job disappear at the end of the day. Work is no longer permitted to leave its paper strewn footprints and gadget trails all over the place and stays contained within allocated spaces in our 3D surroundings, as well as our mind. Limiting objects and the associations they carry to certain areas creates a balance between them. Toys are rebels and refuse to cooperate; they take over the home and make grown up space a scarce commodity. A visitor who comes into the house while the family are out could make an informed guess about gender, age and personal interests of the children while the parents seem to have disappeared into thin air. Favourite objects have been removed to save them from getting broken or scribbled on. 'Toy-ification' of the home can be a symbol for what is happening in real life. Although the job description clearly labels the role as temporary the adults have lost themselves in what feels like 24/7 parenting shifts, putting themselves and their relationship on a backburner. Children are arrows on the way out into their world, drawing their unique flight path into the heavens. If carers shrink their universe to make their life about what the children are up to, there is not enough room for growth for any of the generations involved. Why should a child's bedroom remain untouched years after they have moved out, why should a home consist of playrooms only? Every occupant has the right to an area where they can dedicate themselves to their interests and recharge; a special corner as a springboard into me-time that allows for reconnecting to that mystery of 'I am...' We are so much more than the roles we play.

Our desk can serve as another interesting 'reflector'. A client wondered why colleagues misused his worktop as a dumping ground for migrant files and, in so doing , they were trespassing into far more delicate areas than a square meter of wood. Documents presented an interesting challenge. "How can I become more assertive?" Nobody can overstep boundaries or make us feel inadequate if we are not giving them permission to do so.

If we focus on hoped for applause, everybody's wish turns into our command and we remain forever busy fulfilling requests. Another client had been working in insurance up into his mid-forties. Only after his mother had passed away did he follow his dream and retrain as a teacher. The less dependent we are on someone's approval, the freer we are to love them. We remain forever the children of our parents, still hoping they will smile approvingly on our chosen path long after we have passed ourselves off as adult of the species.

Luckily there is an expiry date for blaming our carers and reality comes along far funkier and more multi-dimensional than the cute little black-and-white silhouette of our expectations. Imagine you had to watch a movie where everything was always fine – you would grab your popcorn and get out in a hurry, away from the dreadful dullness of permanent perfect harmony. Endless sunshine creates a desert, an Arabic saying goes. As it is, our life serves our evolution.

How packed with adventure do we want it to be, this day ahead? Taking up offers by the roadside or settling for plodding along, forever sailing around the storms at half-mast? It takes courage to stay true to ourselves. What sounds more promising? 'I was always 'good' which left little scope for the life story I would have liked to tell.' Or: 'My path was the opposite of straightforward. There were dead ends, more than once I didn't know how to carry on. But overall I enjoyed trekking all of those ups and downs as I followed the fork in the road I had chosen. Every step of the way, I did it my way.' A life without clutter is fully our own.

More often than not things are not what they seem, so let's escape from our storage space enclosures and have a scout around the winding alley-ways off the beaten track. Head tilted until we can make out the acoustic pointers that were drowned out by the random noises of accumulating. We remember what we were always good at, follow the call of our calling. There is no dress rehearsal.

Become aware

Clarity and vision

We were lounging around on the sofa all night and still ended up exhausted. How come? Our energy follows our eyes and we had to keep jumping, visually that is, over stacks of objects calling for attention. Hurdling like this would leave an Olympian exhausted. Intuitively we prefer clear optical lines that allow for an uninterrupted flow which is why we love leafing through magazines, to look at pictures of homes and gardens where every orchid and plumped up cushion has been strategically placed for the sake of the photo shoot. (And until we get there, we keep hoarding these clutter-free-dreamhome sci-fi glossies for inspiration purposes.)

When there is too much going on, we cannot rest and objects cannot shine. Sculptures or paintings do not appreciate constant visual competition, having to jostle for attention with all those other 'carefully selected' items. Art shows depend on the breathing space of white walls, only their backdrop of nothingness allows exhibits to unfold their glory and makes them come alive.

One client's living room featured an array of papers, books and clothes evenly scattered around. He was aware how draining it was to try and do some living in that room. Relaxing was impossible due to being pestered by objects with mute but obstinent requests to be put away. He came up with an idea how to counteract this visual unrest and made an effort to keep the fireplace area immaculate, placing a bunch of white roses centre stage. "*Looking there, I rest my eyes and my mind. It helps me to keep my sanity.*" Creating a focal point or feature wall that gives us pleasure is a brilliant way of giving ourselves an optical break. Like a visual petrol station to fill up and keep the momentum going.

We can suppress the uneasiness caused by carefully created chaos but this effort saps energy that is sadly missing elsewhere. Unused ballasts compress our days into a marathon we volunteered to run in full diving gear. Laughter hardly gets a chance to bubble to the surface and minor complaints rule the roost. Today will be another one of those days that are either too cold/hot, wet/dry, windy/sunny or generally 'hard'. Joy does not fancy being around grumpy mates and clears off.

The following exercise highlights the connection between energy levels and things left undone. Briefly close your eyes and give yourself a clutter rating between one and ten. Number one on the scale equals everything just right; ten marks a 360 degree disaster zone. Jot down the number you arrived at. Then close your eyes again and this time give yourself an energy rating. One stands for super/wo/man, ten is the desire to fall back into bed even before we have peeled ourselves halfway out of the sheets in ultra slow motion. Is there a connection between the results?

A group of walkers wades miserably through the pouring rain, heads down. Suddenly a woman stops. "What can you see?" – "Mud, sludge, dirt." – "What are you going to talk about when you come back? That you have spent a day feasting your eyes with dirt? How about looking upwards? Where treetops are swaying in the wind and clouds are chasing each other and the soaring birds." Clearing is a powerful tool to reshift our focus. The starting point is to rediscover our home, perceiving details consciously again after years of having got used to each other. We turn the key in the door and walk in. What atmosphere is palpable – second-hand shop, stopping-off place? Last stop? What is going on in here, what is not going on? Did we hide the signposts marked 'way out' somewhere in between a few objects too many and embark on a walk around in circles? Spending time in a homemade maze and keeping busy by rearranging the furniture can be a cosier option than risking the way forward which feels so remote, somehow. Photographs help to rediscover the markings; a bedroom snapshot reveals shoe boxes nesting on top of wardrobes and stacks of who-knows-what shooting up in dim corners. Instead of further training in the art of over-looking we get to join the master class of seeing clearly and becoming aware. Let's grab the pen. The next chapter of our life story is waiting in the wings, ready to be outlined, pinned down, manifested.

What have we all got in common? Clutter and dreams. The fascinating thing is that the conscious handling of stuff can turn vague visions into reality. Decluttering makes your dreams come true! How does that sound! Clearing gives us a chance to work hands on with the fascinating universal law when something old leaves, something new comes in – which makes mindless clearing a no-no. Imagine if you ended up with a box of files to get rid of. Then the new comes in and guess what? It turns out to be a brand new box of old files. While sorting through stuff we focus on what it is we are making space for, what we would like to invite into our life. Priority number one is to concentrate on the goodies we are creating a vacuum for, so they can come zooming in: career progression, more time to read, a new friend... If we manage to be clear about the essence we are after – peace and quiet, love, harmony, abundance – there is more leeway for the universe when it comes to manifesting as we have not narrowed our options into specific details. No matter how concise or open-ended, the main thing is that there is a wish. We utilise clutter as a power tool to get from where we are to where we want to be and we brace ourselves for pleasant surprises.

It is inspiring to translate a want into a symbolic action; like inviting good health into the vacuum that is being created with a clearout of the medicine cabinet. If we long for more freedom, the first step could be a desk we can see the surface of, or a home that welcomes spontaneous visitors without a host reeling off apologies and explanations.

Occasionally we end up in a life that is not a lot to do with us anymore. We wake up in a job or a relationship that belongs to a person we no longer are. If we have temporarily boxed up our sense of direction, we ask for clarity when something old leaves. Inspiration for the next step out of the fog reaches us via unlikely routes: snippets of a conversation we overhear on the train, or a sentence that catches our eye while flicking through an online magazine.

We are intimately connected to our home, so every positive change on the outside pushes up our internal bliss quotient. We benefit just as much from any spa treatment we spoil our home with: defoliate with a spot of sanding, then apply moisturiser with creamy licks of paint.

If we do not stay awake, the day to day humdrum will turn us into creatures of habit. They are useful little helpers as long as they assist with driving a car or brushing teeth on autopilot, sparing us from racking our brains, "Hang on, washing hands – where do I start? Turn on tap, apply soap…" However, they tend to sneakily clamber from their space in the car boot of our life into the driver's seat and take over the steering wheel. Creatures of habit reside on the superficial side of things; they never climb high enough to enjoy breathtaking views into possible adventures ahead. They crawl around in the well-known and refuse to paddle out of the shallows, holding us back from sliding over the rainbow to bounce up into a sky that is no longer the limit.

Following a vision prevents us from going nowhere fast. Post-clearing there is less distraction, less numbing, less running away. A plane diverts from the target about 90% of the time, but still arrives at the destination because it constantly adjusts its flight path. If plan A did not work out, stay cool. The alphabet offers 25 more letters to go through.

Clarity empowers us to realign our course, firmly strapped into the driver's seat we remain in control of speed(ing!) and destination. Without goals we resemble the farmer who proudly presented his state of the art machinery, explaining every feature in great detail. When asked about the harvest he fell silent. He had got so distracted by his funky collection of vehicles, so carried away polishing fancy tools that he had all but forgotten to sow the seed. And so there was nothing to harvest.

What are you sowing, what would you like to reap?

Equanimity

According to statistics we live longer than ever, death through illness has reached its lowest level since records began; the same goes for crime statistics. The global income per capita has never been higher, wars and civil wars are in decline. There are more than five times as many democratic nations today as there were in 1950. Still the longing for the 'good old' times, times as beautiful as they never were. Why? Blame the caveman in us. We still react instinctively to events in the same as this reaction saved hunter-gatherers from being eaten. We fear the unknown; anything out of the ordinary could be a threat. The subconscious cannot distinguish between an event being a reality or fiction, which is why we believe in the danger of another tidal wave even if we ended up as lottery millionaires five times over before our toes even got wet. Another challenge is a lack of logic. Would we worry about an alleged new cancer risk if it was 1 in 10 million? Surveys say yes, although we are more likely to be killed by lightning. We rarely question generalising statements in media reports like, "In the future more people will get cancer," which is correct only in as far as there are greater numbers of humans who live longer and age is one of the biggest risk factors. The percentage of cases where the disease ends in death is on the decline.

When we process information we tend to neglect facts and react emotionally instead. Moderate threats only make moderate headlines; the media concentrate on scary but relative risks. Some sections of society have a vested interest in keeping fear levels up: security or research budgets could face cuts if alarm bells did not go off on a regular basis. If it pays insurance companies, NGOs or charities to present facts in dramatic ways, it is not surprising that many people are worried about many things. However, we can get out of the loop with a pair of media blinkers and a readiness to read between the lines.

When it comes to news, apparently only bad news qualifies, whereas good news is deemed unworthy of reporting. There are 'good deed feeds' in newspapers or on websites dedicated to encouraging initiatives to rectify this bias. From every disaster spring inspiring examples of human relief actions, aid and support. Fear waves vibrate down the generations but we can tune into different frequencies anytime we choose to. We were born with just two inherent forms of fear which were installed as life savers: fear of falling from a great height and fear of an unfamiliar loud noise. All other fears have been 'learned' later. The fear of humiliation impacts most visibly on our actions.

Once we have outgrown the 'might come in useful' outlook, we can move on from feeling hard done by because we cannot afford a second designer handbag at present. Hoarding stuff because we are worried about future lackings brings blockages instead of security. "I don't trust life. I know I won't be provided for in years to come and will be forced to make do without a spare tin opener when I most desperately need one." We co-create our reality through cognitive patterns and clearing makes for a fabulous training ground towards an attitude that cultivates trust. "If I should ever require a mug like this again, life will supply something even better." We are staring the fear that is trying to intimidate us yet again in the face . "*Don't* do it. How could you even entertain the thought of chucking this away when you know deep down that it might come in useful at some point? You won't be able to get hold of another pen/rubber band/button/piece of paper/wire like this. Ever," our subconscious says. Well, we did not have the faintest idea in the first place what this wire was meant to do. It was never used and in all likelihood never will be. While we are still pondering, orphaned wire in hand, another fear is approaching. "*Keep it!!* Don't take risks like that. Better be on the safe side, you never know." What are we afraid of? Any fear diminishes as soon as we face it. "If I recycle this bit of paper, I lose access to the information, inspiration and opportunity it represents and will end up as an utter failure. No money, no place to live, no food. Nobody will be there to help me." If we are climbing down those fear cliffs hand over hand several times, we notice that only the beginning varies. In the end it boils down to the same predictable story, "If I give this away, I won't be able to get hold of something similar again. Lose everything, die."

Snap open the handcuffs with keys retrieved from the latest long forgotten box, clear out the 'just in case' mentality once and for all and celebrate with a feast made of stockpiled tins, cans and cartons. We eat our way out, towards a life of spacious kitchen cabinets and walking on air. Off to inspect other secret hoards: stacks of shampoos, weird cleaning products, random sachets and sample packs, nuts without bolts. We get radical and ready for a life beyond 'just in case'. Three backup copies and two sets of spares each are faded out into their new incarnation as nothing but distant memories.

Having exercised our clearing muscle we now feel strong enough to face demons that do not come in pretty boxes. Those wafting about in the background of our consciousness, where they are less easily pinned down to face 'clearageddon'. First up is fear, so destructive because it kills off generosity. As long as we are secretly afraid not to get enough for ourselves – while the proof of the contrary is piling up around us – we will not be truly sharing, but merely donating the odd bit here and there. It is a moral obligation to overcome poverty consciousness; our planet has resources to feed all of humanity. Distribution is where it goes haywire. Conscious clearing helps us approach a less angst-ridden attitude towards hoarding.

At Christmas a family traditionally presents their cats, the dog and the garden birds and squirrels with grains and meats. While they are walking around sharing out treats, the children bring up the fact that people elsewhere would be happy to eat what they are giving to the animals. They decide on a donation. Back in the house the youngest girl empties the contents of her piggy bank onto the dining table, saying she would like to contribute all of it towards the charity fund. When the parents volunteer some notes, the little one protests, "That doesn't hurt you! I was saving up for a pony game and was almost there. Now I have to start waiting all over again and that hurts." The parents debate a more radical contribution on their part and agree to donate the funds that were set aside for a kitchen makeover.

Delayed gratification can make us aware of and even grateful for what we take for granted. Zoom in on another spot on the globe or go back in time to grandmother's life: she ate out twice a year and owned one winter coat, which she wore for a minimum of five years. Her beauty extravagances were a tub of hand cream and a lipstick. As for holidays, there might have been the odd week by the coast every other year, whereas we feel short-changed when we do not get our annual sun or skiing holiday and several mini-breaks. Are we happier than more frugal generations? Not really. Happiness is a state of being that is only randomly connected to the state of having. Give us too much of anything and we stop appreciating it. Pleasure in purchasing has been diminished because it is now a constant. Material goods rarely provide us with sustainable joy. The activities that light up the pleasure centre in the brain are free: cuddles, cycling in the park, a meaningful conversation, seeing friends. We are social creatures, switched into happy mode courtesy of experiences that stimulate our sense of community.

Luckily we never have to worry about giving away 'too much' because the more things, love, money or attention we give away, the more things, love, money or attention will come into our life. If we cannot manage to think back far enough to be able to recall the last time we gave something away, we might have been wondering why life has not showered us with goodies lately. Here is a true story about a woman who ventured out with a plate of food and returned with more than she could carry. The cake had just come out of the oven so she decided to take some over to the neighbours further up the road. While they were chatting by the door, they suddenly remembered, "You have got young children, haven't you? Our kids have outgrown their tricycle and scooter, could you use them for your little ones?"

Fear originated as a protective biological device and is, as such, neither good nor bad. It is a signal rocket that marks the most promising routes. Every time we tap half a tentative toe out of our comfort zone it says hello. As soon as we give in to fear, we limit ourselves. Our name is on the guest list of this gorgeous carnival called life. Joining in is up to us.

Never be afraid of being afraid! The only way to get rid of a fear is to do what scares us. Crocodile jumping? Public speaking? Eating snails? Admitting something to ourselves? One risk a day, bring it on. Even if we end up not enjoying it, we face the challenges of the unknown head on and order the scariest sounding item on the menu. We might end up looking daft but still forge ahead and give that new hairstyle a try. They might not love us back, but we still chat to the person on the seat next to us. It might turn out to be the most disastrous meal in the universe; we still have a go at that recipe. They might turn away; we still take heart and smile at the stranger.

Boosted by these bouts of courage we can be bold and jump over our own shadow, right into the next happiness-opportunity. Clearing our way forward into an attitude that revives itself by taking every single mini-risk going and refuses to join the lukewarm choruses of whinging whys?, crying out *why not?!* instead. No more sitting in a guarded home with a guarded heart, waiting for the lump of gold dropping from the heavens but starting to collect the nuggets all around.

A ship is safest bopping in the harbour, which is not what it was built for. In hindsight, we hardly ever seriously regret what we have done, but feel truly sorry about what we have failed to do. Rewind and start over while there is time. Get in touch with that friend. Start to take dreams more seriously than fears. Pull out the stops, get moving and make some noise.

Intuition

We are trained to live in our head and exclusively rely on our mind for decision making which is not always the most reliable of tools. Anyone who ever opened the Pandora's Box that they had just dragged down from the loft will know that thoughts and feelings attack out of the blue as soon as we open it. Decluttering is a mindboggling undertaking and once we tune in to the Radio Crazy broadcast in our mind we are zapped into the white noise of associations. Conscious clearing reconnects us with a more reliable and overall superior way of decision making. It is a direct line to our gut feeling. Intuition is the wisdom of the heart and a gift all of us have access to. We have been supplied with the antennas, but as we hardly ever put our feelers out they get rusty. Inspiration is ours for the taking if we manage to let it come through. Clearouts are like mouth-to-mouth resuscitation for the sixth sense. Let's get breathing, take up the first object and rest it in our hands. Does it stay or does it go? We switch off the mind and retune from thinking to feeling. Which signals are coming from the gut? An inner warmth, a boost and shudders of happiness all over, like a "Yeahyeahyippiey ippieyeahyeah"singalong instant high? Or is the feeling more like a draining "Oh no" slump? Amazing, isn't it, you did not even have to get yourself down the gym or do a single sit up and still benefit from abdominal exercise: a six-pack as the unlikely side effect of clutter clearing – no end to the surprises it holds in store!

"Does this item recharge me; does it feel in line with my current priorities?" Feelings are the language of the soul. The clearing process awards re-sensitisation for the energy in and behind *every thing*. After the beginner stages of handling objects, we are getting ready to expand the playing field and test out which words, photographs, films, people, thoughts, conversations, music, ideas or ways of doing things recharge us. Our gut as our GPS system and compass rolled into one, pointing south by southwest, leading the way towards the blue skies and green, green grass of feeling at home with ourselves. We *get in touch* with why we choose some actions over others and begin to develop a sense of why we do things. Is it because we are hoping to get someplace else at some point or are we doing it because it feels good right now?

Our inner voice is always a peace messenger. It might ask for attention when we go for a third espresso but deny ourselves strawberries on the side. Intuition loves whispering understated trifles like, "Go that way, walk in there. Sit down over here." It issues warnings to bite our tongue, "Don't say that, try this instead." It challenges us not to withhold praise, to turn on the light switch and flood our surroundings with fluorescent encouragement. "Would you please give my regards to the chef, the food was superb. And the service excellent, no surprises there." An impulse to say or do something nice is easy to ignore, "This colour really suits her, pay a compliment!" but if we manage to become aware of the inspirational whispers and then follow through, wellbeing-thermometers of everyone involved shoot up into a pleasant warmth.

We might have clocked up the birthday numbers that mark us as official members of the adult generation but we still have to contend with aspects of our personality that refuse to grow up. Is that the inner child peepingout? In the clearing process we get to listen to quite a few of our inner voices and meet the characters they belong to: the know it all, the inner critics and saboteurs, the victim... How about holding a team meeting with those archetypes to maximise their diverse talents? If our fear-afflicted tightwad murmurs something about not spending that much money on a present, or urges us to rush past the hat of a street musician; we smile inwardly, reassuring both him and ourselves, "Don't worry, *the more I give, the more I will receive* – law of the universe!" We invite something into our live by giving something else away.

So when are we grown up then? Maturity is a balance between daring and consideration, spiced up by a cheeky dose of recklessness. The inner rogue still gets to stop by every now and again and we have not deposited all of our intrepidness at the cloakroom and then misplaced the ticket. We no longer have to prove our worth; intuition and intellect work as a team; confidence is built on integrity and we know what feels good and right for us and follow through. Inner messages have become clear enough to fade out the medley of opinions from the outside. We set ourselves free when we have taken a break from being the centre of the universe; when we know in our heart what our truth is and are no longer afraid of speaking it. When we acknowledge clarity and truth as liberating powers that move life forward.

Patience and self-discipline

Clutter clearing never ends. Luckily, as you surely hasten to add, as otherwise all those positive side effects would disappear as well. (Imagine going back to a life without intuition or a six pack?) Continuous action is required, regular twenty minute-sessions instead of an elusive tour de force at the weekend. Annoyingly, we will not declutter years of passionate accumulating in an afternoon session. Of course we had hoped to be done with sorting through clothes or books after round two at the latest, but now find ourselves revisiting wardrobe and bookcase for the fifth time – which is when we get introduced to the relations of creativity: discipline and patience. Going through hole-punched page after hole-punched page with the patience of a saint and – zap – another fat lever arch file has disappeared into thin air. Doing what we can, with what we have, where we are. Hitting that reply button and taking up the receiver, saying yes, saying no, staying on track and refusing to give up just because something becomes hard. Optimism is the most important renewable energy source and is produced by the ABC-technique. A for allow, permitting ourselves to experience happy moments. B for begin, what can I do right now? C stands for: carry on – never give up, never surrender! Demolish the paper stalagmites on the desk in the seventeenth session. Consistent small changes eventually lead onto the open top coach of the champions' parade.

> *"As I made my way through each room, I was amazed by what I found. I couldn't believe I had 'saved' so much! Each time I threw something out I imagined that I was letting go of old stuff that was keeping me stuck. Over time, as my home became less and less cluttered, I noticed that I had more space for friends, experiences and opportunities. I can't tell you how often letting go of a box of old books or files led to a new business opportunity or friendship.*

Decluttering was a year-long process that completely changed my life. I got so used to being rewarded when I let go of things that held old energy that it became a kind of game."

We adore the eventful phases in our life where we zoom forward, results coming in so thick and fast we can watch ourselves grow. Clearing can teach us to appreciate the plateau stages, those indescript states of being where we seem to be forever circling without land in sight. These are the times to assimilate experiences; we grow more patient and calm (except when we forget.) Just for a moment on two, we can feel it in our bones that the journey is the destination, that life happens in moments and moments do not care what time it is. We get to remember what toddlers have not yet forgotten: how to stay in the now and remain centred withinourself. Of course they choose to demonstrate this enviable skill when we are rushed off our feet. Yep, agreed, the journey is the destination but, "Come on!!" We hurry the child along, the latest to-dos spinning through our mind while the little one drives us round the bend, up the wall and other places we never intended to get acquainted with, taking (what feels like) hours to make it halfway down the road. It is impossible to rush if you are interested in every pebble on the way. If you have to touch all those amazing twigs and leaves and feathers and lift up your treasures for closer inspection, toddling back every now and again because you have spotted another stick that could turn out to be even more fascinating. If you refuse to get sidetracked by appointments ahead. Clearing invites us back into camping out in slow motion where we can hear butterflies giggling and know what clouds taste like.

IV Clearing secrets revealed: where to start and how not to stop!

This is chapter four, the dawn of a new era. Day one on the all clear calendar: on your marks, get set, lighten your load! We did try to make a start and fished photographs or clothes out of respective boxes to distribute them carefully all over the floor. What happened next was not intended. Instead of an organising session we ended up with a miniature panic attack, frantically gathering everything together to squash it back into the darkness it had emerged from. Slammed the lid back on, phew. Ready, steady, stay where you are?

You are probably convinced you are the only person on the planet who ever experienced this but guess what, exactly this happens to all of us when the project is too ambitious. Roughly 99% of clueless clearing hopefuls underestimate the power of things, thinking they can just jump into the vast ocean of memories head first. Paddling like crazy we flag SOS, get us out of here. Feelings flood in; we stem them with dams made of boxes. Objects are great pretenders. They pose as harmless everyday stuff but they are gate keepers for complex, often downright awkward and always tricky things. They have even been caught – on several occasions – inflating themselves into issues!

So now we have established that it is not you and you are not crazy and we are all in the same boat. Clearing is doable and afterwards we feel so much lighter; less troubled by our stuff. Good news from a class member *"I would never have believed how this decluttering/refining really lightens and brightens people's lives."*

So – where do we start, how do we keep going? Occasionally we hit the bull's eye in the shape of a deadline looming large: the landlord, the estate agents, the in-laws are due a visit or a new arrival will soon be claiming some of our precious space. We have a big birthday coming up or want a potential buyer to turn into a genuine one. If deadlines do the trick we make one up. In a home that feels small we will end up with a life that feels the same. Let's reclaim some space along with the spring in our step and the free spirit we used to be before we got tied down in stuff.

How long does it take to make a start? "On Saturday I'll tackle the loft." The weekend comes and goes and the loft has lost out yet again. Watching the telly, watching paint dry, going out or all of the above passed themselves off as more attractive options. And here is how to make it work: keep the project manageable. Start small, or even better: tiny. It is too overwhelming to wrestle with the entire contents of a wardrobe or bookshelf. The secret to success is to limit ourselves to one straightforward miniature task at a time: one file, one row in a shelf, ten items or ten minutes. No more. We treat ourselves to a mini-clearout and the joys that come with it (free delivery!) Feelings of being in control, headed for freedom and serene calm.

Where we start does not matter. Pondering the whereabouts at length – kitchen, cupboard, cabinet – is just another thinly veiled procrastination technique and a waste of what could be precious clearing time. Anywhere is great. The Feng Shui Bagua (see bonustrack page XY) can help to find a starting point. Ask yourself which area of your life could do with a boost right now and get going in that corner, be it career or relationship. Alternatively, tackle a small section that annoys you; all time classics being the cupboard under the sink or the dining table littered with paperwork. Another option is to start where it feels least difficult. One client came up with the idea of going through the drinks cabinet and enjoyed the satisfying feeling of pouring away the dregs to end up with a lively mini-bar ready for the next impromptu celebration. Another client cleared out the wardrobe and drawers in the spare room and surprised her visiting cousin with plenty of space to put things away so she could delight in the relaxing surroundings of a welcoming guestroom.

If you enjoy symbolic action: cellars stand for the past and the unconscious, the loft for future and self-development; where are the current blockages or priorities?

Once we have taken the where-hurdle, the next stumbling block is the when. How soon is soon? When is the best time? Whenever. There are only two days in a year when we cannot do any clearing: one is yesterday, the other is tomorrow. We would not say to a friend, "Let's meet up once I find the time." We make an appointment with ourselves and put the first ten minutes in the diary for Monday at 7.30pm. And then we show up. No more phantasising about a week off when we will get everything done perfectly. Arguments for 'doing this properly' are safely packed away where they belong: in the realm of utopia. Pretty phrases like, "I just don't like doing things by halves, you know" are excuses to have another go at our procrastination game. Perfectionism hampers action. How about admitting to ourselves that the urgent wish for an uninterrupted block of time just prolongs the state of inertia? "I'll think it all over on holiday."

Yeah, right. Real life does not queue up to patiently wait last in line for the next annual leave to come around. It pulsates in intervals, one week of which offers more than 1000 opportunities for ten minute appointments. As Mickey Mouse phrased it so succinctly, "It's a brand new day – what are you waiting for?!"

As for being in the right mood to tackle a clearing project; any old mood will do. Sitting around waiting for an ideal state of mind or extra high spirits to turn up does not count. If it never qualified as one of our all-time favourites to tick our way down the to-do-list, the chances are it will not happen anytime soon, even if we are hanging in there for another week. Anger, tears or any state of minor upset are great to get started because we will be chucking out junk left, right and centre.

So we have got ourselves a date. It might be with a box and a bag but, of course, we dress up and put on comfy clothes in our favourite colours. Anything motivating is invited to join the party. Music keeps us company, cheering us on should stamina temporarily evaporate. And of course we call on our good old friends the bribes with rewards at half time (treat) and after successful completion (cinema ticket) of the clearing project.

Decluttering is often misunderstood as a synonym for reshifting. Of course not by you, dear reader, who is now part of the in-crowd and able to decipher slogans like 'create some space in your life!' to mean 'waste your money on our storage!' Plonking down boxes in a commercial rental unit, or skilfully creating one big stack out of two smaller ones does not qualify as clearing. The symptoms of pseudo-decluttering can be diagnosed when the essential step of 'getting rid of' has gone missing in the piles somewhere. When even prolonged efforts of moving things from pillar to post do not reward us with improved structure and focus there is no organising happening. Sorry. But here is the good news: you might have been determined not to part with any item whatsoever (books are a classic for that one) but once you get started you still end up lightening your load, as if by default. One of my clients insisted on organising hundreds of books without seeing one of them leave the premises. Once the sorting got underway he came across numerous identical copies, discovered unwelcome presents of which he had not even read the dust jacket of, dug out study and reference books that were utterly out of date. In the end the living room featured massive stacks of printed paper that he was more than happy to be rid of. Moral of the story: things which are ready to leave make their way to the door almost by themselves.

Try to get a feel for what works best for you. Do you prefer to sort standing up or sitting down at the desk, lounging on the sofa or next to the meditation corner? You are the expert. If you are unhappy with the state of a whole room or large area, it is best to take the items you want to work on away from that space altogether as it emanates confusion. Grab a bag, fill it up, retreat into a sanctuary you feel comfortable in and see your success rate rocket.

It is a great idea to make ourselves accountable and brag about plans for ambitious mammoth projects to diminish the temptation of chickening out last minute. Once we feel ready to up the ante and plan for a longer session, our allies are bags labelled rubbish, recycling, charity, to do (return, have repaired, dry cleaned etc).

A transit box houses vagrants that got themselves lost. The stray corkscrew is not taken back to the kitchen straight away as there is a slim chance we might get sidetracked into putting the kettle on or dream up other fabulous distractions. Lost items are reunited only at the end of the session which leaves temptation out high and dry – we are currently not available as its victims, too busy. A dilemma box helps with problematic stuff. Before we get muddled up in the mental to and fro, the item gets chucked in the box without further ado. Reaching a verdict happens all by itself. If we rush back to the box within twenty minutes (which felt like an eternity) to rip off the lid, retrieve the dearly missed object, clutch it against our chest trembling all over and cry out, "How could I survive without you?!" decision made. On the other hand, if in weeks to come the situation develops along the lines of, "What thingummy did I put in that box again..?" the contents are on their way towards more appreciative owners.

A fundamental principle is to clear from the inside out. The starting point is not the top of an overcrowded desk but its guts. We have to weed through drawers first to free up space for what we want to keep. Our papers are freed from their nomadic way of life where they were forced to roam the home, forever on the lookout for a place to settle. We avoid mega messes and never pull out everything at once; it gets more chaotic anyway before clarity rises up like a phoenix from the heaps. We warm up with the items we find easiest, slowly progressing to trickier challenges like presents or photographs.

Be warned: class members reported that once you have acquired a taste for the therapeutic effects of the mini-clearout, getting past the front door without another little bag to drop off at the charity shop becomes almost impossible. We find ourselves pacing the premises on the lookout for more items that have outstayed their welcome – *the High of Letting Go* turns old and young alike into persistent offenders!

Then for the handy work. One object after another has to pass with a resounding *yes!* to at least one of these questions: "Do you make me feel good? Am I using you?" With every item undergoing the test run we get further away from contemplating the *where*abouts and advance towards the more profound and truly tricky grounds of, "*Why* am I keeping you? Are you still about me or about where I want to be headed?" Mugs make brilliant tour guides. Courtesy of things we had forgotten about, we conquer peak after peak and are presented with brand new outlooks.

"I just do two water melons a day," is how one client described her clearing technique. As she did not want to be distracted by checking the time once she had started a session, she set her alarm and put it inside a slice of watermelon, a colourful plastic pouch in the shape of her favourite fruit. She worked away at a project trusting in her friendly melon to let her know when it was time to stop. Play around with session lengths and formats until you find what works for you.

Did you mean to set up a folder with travel ideas or a health file but everything is full up? You probably have some paper dinosaurs dating back to the years at uni hogging the bottom shelves. Still fondly attached to the Stone Age relics of an eventful past as a whale saving activist or a fundraising queen of the PTA? "We had such a great time back then. In my days..." Those days are still ticking along nicely. Paper collections can be slimmed down to a 'best of': seven folders turning into three, three into one, et voilà there is space for the new. Would you rather live in a shrine to the past or enjoy a present sparkling with promise? Things trapped in storage boxes are highly suspect. How did they get in there? Probably because all available seats in the home are already taken by stuff that is more appreciated. Release the box exiles from the darkness and let them get a life. Clearing helps us to think 'out of the box' better than any brainstorming session ever could.

> *"I am on a roll again! I can't believe that after the last 2 years of clearing out there is still so much more to go. I did a boot sale at the weekend to get rid of some of my stuff and some of Mum's. We made a bit of money but I'm not sure it's worth the aggravation. I was planning on doing another boot sale with the stuff that was left but we packed up afterwards and something clicked. I just didn't want to take it back to the house. So I called a friend who does boot sales for charity and we went straight round there and gave it all to her. – Since then I have been a woman possessed! I can't wait to get home from work to do some more sorting out. I have another car load of stuff for my friend and I'm still going. I am starting to get concerned that, once I have got rid of all the stuff that I never use, there won't be much left!"*

The need to fill a space on the outside results from the need to fill an empty space inside. Clutter is a distraction we have to gently wean ourselves off. It takes time to get used to the new 'minimalism' that feels like bareness XXXL, a few extras too large and downright scary. Letting go means leaving the fields of gravity behind and drifting off into a space with precious little to trip over and nothing to hold on to. As long as we stay stuck we are not in danger of plunging into an abyss. Taking down the clutter walls means kicking off our crutches, while simultaneously donating the security blanket. We remember our recently acquired virtue of patience and help ourselves to a generous dose.

Clearing time is body clock time. We hold hands with every object in question, nothing forced, hurried, fast or furious. Even if it would spell quick relief, we resist the temptation of dumping a box without looking through the contents. It only takes a few minutes now but could get us stuck forever in a mental glue-trap where we are wondering regretfully, "That didn't have ... in it, did it?"

Clearing is reorganising. Everything finds a permanent home; items that are used regularly get to reside in the most accessible places. The exasperated exclamation, "This property just hasn't got enough storage space!" must renounce its 'reasonable' status because nine out of ten times it is about space not used effectively. Believers of this myth are masters of blocking prime storage areas with things that are hardly used and would be better off sitting in a shed or loft. (Alright, those are full. So our 'from the inside out' principle comes in handy again. Note to self: spaces that are required to house itinerant objects make yet another fabulous starting point.)

How much long-distance running is going on from detergent to washing machine, from flower to vase, from dishwasher to cabinet?

Things that are related get to flat-share the same storage spaces. When you start to feel flustered or overwhelmed, hold on to your hat, take off and switch into bird's-eye view. A sobering and much loved exercise from class is to think about what we would take if there was a fire or we had to flee. One participant chose his mobile phone only. "I've got all my contacts in there; I could literally call for help." Another class member shared that this was not just a mind game but had actually happened to her family when she was seven years old. Someone else told us about how she suddenly woke up one night, the house was on fire. Her husband was carrying a child and the document folder. She held the other child in her arms, one hand left to grab hold of something else. She let her eyes wander, split seconds, "What am I going to take?" when it hit her, "I already have everything I need."

What would you drag from the flames with your bare hands?

Fine feathers make fine birds

The 80/20 rule also applies to stuff; we utilise 20% of our belongings 80% of the time. Statistics translate as: we use a few things constantly, forget about the rest. When it comes to clothes, we never get out of our favourite outfits while all the other beauties are pining away buried in the darkness of the wardrobe, longing for their next outing. Like all objects, clothes make great storytellers. They speak of our changing shapes, of holidays, weddings and funerals. Why hang on to costumes of past plays and long forgotten shows while we are already starring in a brand new production? It started this morning, blinds up and ready to take the curtain call.

Putting on clothes that make us feel below par is an unnecessary energy expense. We keep tugging and pulling and worrying if it is too tight, too low cut or too see-through. Is the seam showing, does my bum look a bummer in this..? Thinking about what others might think costs life-juice, wearing items that feature holes or stains is putting on a suit made of insecurity. When our clothes feel tired and worn out it rubs off on us. Wellness-inducing outfits uplift us which means only clothes that fit properly are permitted to stay. If in doubt, check with your old friend and foe, the mirror and team up with your new ally gut feeling. With those helpers by our side, what does wearing feel like, "If I pull in my tummy I might be alright," or "Wohoo!"? Underestimate the feel-good factor of clothes at your peril, wearing outfits that make us ready to take on the world can be incredibly empowering. Clothes can also help us to break new ground and grow into an unfamiliar role or newly adopted image. Business, arts, academics – red scarf, bow tie, pumps, suit and trainer combo; have fun trialling the dress codes of different worlds.

We wander the streets in baggy pants while our Sunday best is patiently suffocating in the dry-cleaning plastic we promised to take it out of once the special event had arrived. Unbeknownst to us, it is already here. The rest of our life starts today, how is that for an occasion. Fine feathers make fine birds but only if given a chance to beautify the body they were bought for. Clothes cannot wait to finally be the chosen one, to put in an appearance and see the light of day! No more limiting beliefs and excessive compartmentalisation: this is to be worn at home, this for DIY, this for going out. Items are worn again, born again anytime now; we strut out onto the globe in high heels – high tea here we come.

A wardrobe full of sales items could be an inspiration to stop 'snapping up' reduced pieces that try to pass themselves off as bargains. From now on, we only purchase items that make us feel one in 7 billion every time we step out. We might be afraid of parting with unloved clothes because we fear an empty wardrobe. Imagine life after the edit: no more panicky ransacking, getting angry, running late but swinging the doors open to find our most beloved treasures in pride of place. Beautiful recharging vibes from a splendour of colours and fabrics.

Here is the wardrobe action plan that makes this vision sound less like science fiction and rewards us with the pleasure of dipping into a treasure chest instead of rummaging through a conservation area: pass on anything that cannot boast the feel-good factor. No worries if it is not in pristine condition, charities are happy to accept donations unfit for resale as they receive funds for fabric recycling. Sorting is done in sections to keep feelings of being overwhelmed at bay. Shirts only to start with, if even a single category is too large it gets broken down further for example, into colours. Another approach is to revisit the 'ten items at a time' strategy.

We have to try on every piece we are not sure about because clothes are tricksters. They specialise in looking fabulous – to suddenly stop doing so when we put them on. They love playing that game in shops, looking incredibly funky and sleek on the hanger and – let's paraphrase it as – slightly less stunning once we are wearing them. Trying things on one last time is also a way of saying goodbye. "Thanks for being such a gorgeous pair of trousers, we had memorable times together. Bye bye now."

Updating a list of items that have left – 28 books, 7 pairs of shoes, 11 shirts – gets us out of the danger zone of being swallowed up by the delusional, "But I haven't achieved anything yet," letdown that seems to be the weirdo companion tagging along with every successful clearout.

"Hi, just a quick PROGRESS report (note capital letters!) This is the result so far for the pieces of clothing that were pulled out of boxes: definitely keep: 3; maybe keep: 19; GONE: 57 – not bad!!! – Tonight I am going out to a posh dinner and will be dressed up to the nines in one of my new old dresses!"

What would we want to invite into the vacuum that has been created by parting with clothes? A client shared how she asked for the ability to be accepting and appreciative of her body every time she walked to the charity shop with another bag of dazzling dresses that did not fit anymore. She had clung to the clothes because their size and style symbolised her youth, a time and body gone by. Letting go of the dresses she set herself free from holding on to an idealised image of her 21-year-old former self. It brought back what she had chosen not to remember before: that she had never truly felt at ease with her figure or at home in her body, even as that youthful self she was now grieving for. Passing on ill-fitting clothes had become a therapeutic process of accepting herself.

Next step: any items in need of dry cleaning or alterations wait next to the front door to be taken care of and then come back in a wonderfully refreshed state. They move into a wardrobe organised according to categories and colours, now featuring unheard of outfits created by matchmaking: previously untried combinations of trousers, top and accessory get to live on the same hanger, saving us time when we need to be ready in a hurry.

Why do fabrics have to be either black, pinstriped or a particularly dull shade of grey, brown or blue to qualify as 'professional'? Who said we had to go on a colour diet just because we work at a desk? Defiantly, we feed our soul on speckles of pink in a tie, assault the senses with a turquoise handbag, accessorize in neon only and start a revolution. Blissfully unaware of the fashion police, we run riot and introduce outrageous shades of green and purple into the offices of this world.

What do you feel like today? Bask in the rays of the palette: green creates balance and harmony, supports healing and aliveness. Red anchors motivation, action and accomplishment. Pink has uplifting qualities; it vibrates with enthusiasm and love of life. Orange carries creativity, fun and self-confidence. Turquoise grounds us; helps us find inner peace and connection to ancestry. Blue is calming and symbolises focus, truth and integrity. Purple supports vibrations of abundance and inner strength. White carries frequencies of clarity and purity. Yellow stands for hope and joy and increases feelings of self-worth. Is today a yellow day or does it look like an orange one?

Any discussion about clothes sooner or later touches on the topic of weight with related issues of eating, overeating or not eating looming large. Often we cling to items because we insist on kidding ourselves that we could squeeze back into those skinny jeans in three (to thirteen) months time. Meanwhile, we are broadcasting a message to body and self, "I don't accept you as you are." When our thinking revolves around kilos and body shapes only, it might be an invitation to dig deeper. Accomplices on our excursion away from the surface could be books, self-help communities or online forums, whatever works for us. Deep rooted fears lose much of their power when held up into the light of conscious awareness.

What is a priority, sensual delights or a certain number on the size label? Of course we do not just eat because we are hungry. We eat because we are looking for stimulation, we want to come alive, feel alive when we overdose, overwork, overdo it. When the heat is on and we are starring in the lead role of that latest instalment of the drama of the everyday. As human beings we are looking to steer clear of pain and explore higher levels of consciousness and we have had centuries to figure out which substances assist with takeoff and landing. Alcohol lessens fear; tobacco weakens feelings of anger and frustration, sugar as a love substitute, chocolate as an antidote to feelings of separation or loneliness. Nutrition overload or restriction as protective devices; overworking helps to avoid intimacy; excessive consumption of screens suffocates creativity. Handling legally available stimulants and tranquilizers presents us with an exquisite chance to become aware of needs that have gone underground. Clearing brings them back up, decluttering on the level of feelings, especially those that are easiest to spot in others. Substance or behaviour of choice are clues to what we are after when we OD on working, shopping, exercising, anything.

Try this: take a raisin into your hand, the last thing you will ever eat. Roll it between your fingers, feel the fine lines, the juices and the stored up sun that the drying process has locked in. The raisin hits your tongue, unleashes the golden warmth of summer into your mouth. Explode the senses with a bite; chew on energy courtesy of a tiny bit of fruit.

Research confirms that how we feel while we are eating can be as important as what we eat. Feeling states impact on the body's ability to convert nutritional value. Forcing down a salad in a foul mood is bad news for vitamins & Co; they will have a hard time doing us good. Smacking our lips in delight and enjoying one of those treats that have not been exclusively made of raw organic vegetables does not have to be a shortcut to ruining our health. Attitude is a decisive factor: eating, drinking or doing that fire-breathing dragon without feeling guiltily bad about it is better for us. Being aware of a health conscious lifestyle without negating all joys of sensual pleasure where self-prescribed fitness regimes turn into an additional stress factor. Determined to turn into an athlete by tomorrow afternoon, we have to keep checking on recommended units of water, oxygen, mineral or carbohydrate intake while trying not to lose count of our five a day. If we just are what we eat we had better stay away from nuts. Others will notice a few pounds more or less only if *we* insist on declaring it Top Priority. First impressions are all about vibes. "Great guy, a bit short though." "Great guy, he's got amazing eyes as well." Same body dimensions carried off in different ways result in correspondingly varied recordings on inner radars.

Clothes are great tools to feel at home in our body. Size labels are as reliable as lottery numbers but there are flattering cuts and patterns available for all shapes. Obsessing about a few inches more or less on the bum, tum or whichever area we elected to fret about today, is to deny the gift of life. Taking a turn at the monkey game, juggling the gift-of-life-diamond as if it was a stone. We have been given this glorious boneshaker of a body to ride around in for a few decades. A short lifetime long, we can make the most of its stunning features. One hundred trillion cells instantly communicate with one another so we may walk, see, run, laugh, cry, spin, think, taste, trip, fall, get up, perspire, hear, swim, giggle, hug and be hugged. Our bodies are temporary shelters for our soul and clothes horses only on a part-time assignment. Their full-time job is being an energy field. Even if our scales will never get it, we are made of nothingness, of swinging, pulsating vibes. The space in between atoms is almost a hundred times bigger than the atoms themselves.

We are a microcosmic miniature of the universe. Limited special collector's edition, that is.

Conquering the paper mountains

Paper is reassuringly finite with four sides and as many corners and comforting in its permanence. We can hold hands with it, caress it while turning pages. The unfathomable floods of the internet refuse to do that. Clipping and printout cut incessant streams of information into rectangular white breathers that we can handle. Until we are losing it again, that precious overview we fought for with cleverly devised systems of in-trays, e-notes and lever arch files. The relentless greed of printers and copiers gobbles up clarity when they churn out ever more dead wood, kept busy by our gluttony for knowledge, inspiration and those extra copies, just in case.

Paper is a symbol for information and future options. A woman attended a clearing seminar because both she and her husband could not bear the thought of recycling their newspapers before they had double-checked them for relevant articles and info titbits. Stacked up bundles of yesterday's news were encroaching on their living space and causing extra expenses when taken on holiday in an additional suitcase as lines to be read instead of written.

In case you were smiling just now, what are you big on? Carrier bags anyone, used envelopes, empty boxes, plant pots? Hands up if you belong to the contemporary tribe of virtual hoarders digging apps, tunes and followers?

Forms and bills waiting to be dealt with, contact details that need organising as they are currently flying about on random notepad pages – annoying print like that springs to mind when we think of paper clutter. But let's start with the category that weighs in heaviest. We are in awe of books. Their history takes us back to the first scholars who composed handwritten copies of holy knowledge. In book burnings they epitomize freedom of speech and human rights. Here is a suggestion how to demystify our relationship to books: dump one in the bin. For test purposes only, promise! Half a split-second later you can rescue it again. Did the thought make you shiver with disgust? A book is paper with words on it, just like a pizza leaflet. It is not necessarily wisdom distilled into print just because it was graced with a cover. We associate books with knowledge, a changeable commodity indeed: 1500 years ago everybody knew the earth was the centre of the universe. 500 years ago everybody knew the earth was flat. Books are of course far more than carriers of content; they become friends over time, always there to inspire, distract or entertain. They might even replace real relationships. Would you like to own a lively library to dip into or status symbol bookshelves, a colourful but otherwise pretty dead sculpture? We create space for new ideas once we let our old companions go. That none of our books belongs to us is a fact that conveniently slips our mind. They are borrowed for a limited time from the library of life and sooner or later we have to return them all. Join the campaign against the unfair imprisonment of books and set them free!

How much of our lifetime do we want to set aside to fine-tune clippings? The bigger the mountains of the unresolved, the bigger the burden. Dispose of the unfit paper raft, we will not be able to sail away from transience on our makeshift life savers. And while we are at it: how many hours would it take to listen to every single one of our music tracks or watch all of our hoarded movies just once? Every day sees new releases. Why hang on to old love letters if we could pen brand new ones and enrapture currently beating hearts? Only the most glorious highlights in card form survive, in anticipation of those that will come fluttering along, we let the rest join in on the good cause of saving the lives of trees. While fiddling with documents that make us sneeze, it pays off to eavesdrop on our self-talk that features plenty of doing words in the past tense. "Those were good times, everything made sense. That was such an interesting seminar." How about, "These are pretty good times, a lot makes sense at the moment. I'm looking forward to this seminar tomorrow, can't wait. Actually, I've started thinking about doing a talk myself."

Sometimes we enjoy reading gossip; probably because we are compassionate creatures who love to participate in the fates of others. Another reason might be that reports of 'celebrity' troubles provide us with some sort of weird energy boost, like a mini-power-injection. "They have relationship/weight/self-esteem issues like me. Ha." If we swap those short-lived highs for a truly invigorating read we recharge ourselves with more durable inspiration.

Do you derive brownie-point-collecting gratification out of dutifully toiling through a book? "It was a present; I have bought/started this, therefore I have to finish it. Besides, one should have read that." Ho hum – long live freedom of choice! Be brave and rebel against the dictatorship of reading lists and specialist literature. Bury yourself in the unprescribed and revel in your new incarnation as advocate of the hedonist subspecies of the guilt-free pleasure reader.

The latest edition of the magazine thumps through the door and we have not looked at the previous one yet. The piles are sending their familiar Morse code. "Hi!? We would like to inspire and inform you. Yes you! Haven't got the time? Of course. Just leaf through quickly then, in case you wanted to save anything?" We did not know what we were letting ourselves in for when we first committed and signed up. To delight in a subscription is more complicated than we thought. If in doubt get out of the long-term relationship and cancel. Stock up at your local letter dealer when you feel like it or pick up the ad-hoc affair at the station kiosk.

Our energy follows our eyes, quite literally while we are reading. Clearouts sensitise for vibrations behind and beyond print. What is a draining read, what fires us up?

The desk reborn as an oasis of calm

Disclaimer: this header is not ironic – an ideal work environment inspires and recharges. So much for the theory which is a bit like Shakespeare, great when thou understandeth it. Luckily, once we hit practice and resume the Sisiphus undertaking that is clearing a desk we can do without tombs titled '225 easy steps to an organised office' because we have good old common sense to fall back on. How do you know that a file needs breaking down? It is bursting at the seams. And if you spot a consumptive specimen that is down to its last three sheets, they go in with another file – ta dah – first one freed up! Resist temptation to pop into a stationer to buy tons of *really* useful items to 'prepare' for a clearing session. Adhering to the 'from the inside out' principle we will be showered with empties.

Which essence do you collect in paper? Do you get high on hoarding information and future opportunities or are you just trying to insure yourself against mistakes? When the filing spawns quicker than we can buy new storage units, chances are our friend, "That might come in useful one day..." is to blame. And until that 'one day' arrives, we put the snippet here 'for now'. From this moment onward, every sneaky 'for now' sets off the clutter alarm bells in our head as those harmless little words mark a major stumbling block that leaves us stranded in confusion. We have sussed them out now, those bits of paper, once they have crept in they make themselves at home in their favourite spots on tabletops, radiator covers, mantelpieces and any other remotely horizontal surface. No leaflet or envelope gets to sneak past the relentless bouncer we have become, chucking any remotely unnecessary dead wood straight into the recycling box.

Although we remain ever hopeful of being living proof of the opposite; decisions do not come easier if they are postponed for longer. If you are one for handling paper a minimum of ten times until it is dealt with, have fun with the measles test: one dot in the corner every time we grab the sheet, fiercely determined to fill it in or send it off – to drop it again, exasperated. How sick is the poor note in the end? How much energy was lost by launching into the action and then failing halfway through?

Mastery of life is mastery of the moment. Paper is a great confidence coach, holding our hands while rustling reassuringly, "Repeat after me: in case I need this information again, I'll be able to get hold of it in an updated and therefore much more useful version." Trees are our role models. Storms make them take deeper root and come autumn they take the plunge and let go of their leaves, their sustenance, trusting that another spring is on its way. We can be just as brave, out with every single leaf of the just-in-case-keepsake variety. Why rummage through piles of dusty documents if we are only a mouse click away from dozens of relevant links?

The basic clearing principle remains the same in an office space: always work from the inside out. Shuffling up another neat looking stack would be much quicker and look alright, well, better than it does now – and is the fast lane to a dead end. We have to get all of the skeletons out of filing cabinets first. Only essentials like computer or telephone go back as permanent residents of desk land. Paper is organised into categories like recycling, to be read, to do (urgent/long-term), filing (known/unknown) and then tackled with the three-step-technique: do, delegate or file. Zone One (in reach without having to start walking around) is reserved for items that we handle on a daily basis. The less often we use a document, the further away it can be stored.

Here is a trick to feeling exhausted, nervous and overwhelmed even before we have booted up. Just put everything that requires attention right in front of you, ideally in a messy pile that keeps sliding off the desk. Antidote: to-do-documents move into the no longer bottomless in-tray, top drawer or nearby shelf. Future jams are prevented with a system that accommodates favourite hoarding habits: files for recipes, travel ideas or upcoming events.

Farewell to all notes and post-its on the loose; scribbles go straight into the one surviving diary. The note book is freed from its dreary job as list carrier and gets to reinvent itself as inspiration treasure chest. Quotes that give us wings, eureka-moments and doodles have found a new home. We open our gem when we feel like a recharge and nose around in our sparkly collection of those jewels called words, our very own inexhaustible source of magic.

We notice micro-successes and enjoy them; focus on what we have achieved instead of what there is still to do. With every bit of paper gone, every message deleted, we get more of our oomph back. High spirits are coming to party.

Photographs as bringers of joy

We had hoped digitalisation would simplify that tricky business of what to do with all those photographs. Instead we end up taking even more because the sunset might look better from yet another angle. We were going to choose the best and delete the rest at some point, soon, when there is time. Now we are in charge of storing all 27 sunsets and even expected to look at them while last year's holiday pictures are still lurking on the memory stick, demanding to be dealt with. Our get out clause is a change of strategy where we redefine the concept of an album and declare any screen to be a fabulous one. Members of the paper-loving tribe avoid fiddling with photo corners and time-consuming design decisions and slot the pictures into slip-in albums. Another option is emailing them to an online-service that will send back ready-made calendars or photo books.

We take pictures to stop the clock, make time stand still, freeze a memory. We want to conserve key moments, preserve the happy times and define our identity via unique storyboards. "Look at this great holiday / oufit / childhood!" The proof is in the picture. Photographs are feelings squared, they get right through to our heart, documenting history on both grand and sandpit-sized scales. We are as much in awe of pictures as we are worshippers of books, throwing them away seems taboo. It feels disrespectful towards those that have gone before us to leave their yellowing albums behind at the next move. We might be afraid of tossing the memory out with the picture but it was the experience that made us into who we are today, not the print of it. 'Losing' a memory is not possible. We are not throwing people away if we do not hang on indefinitely to every single one of their photos. This is *our* life. Things were created to be used, people to be loved. When we get besotted with things something has gone topsy-turvy.

> *"We talked about photos a few times; they are one of the most difficult things to get rid of. Probably because we think we might forget places/people/experiences without them to remind us. It's an interesting subject. I came across a box of photos and two huge albums that were bulging at the seams. As ever, I started off thinking that I would have to buy another album. But no!! I decided to throw some away. Funny, once I'd decided that, it wasn't that difficult. I had reams of photos from holidays 30 years ago, photos of people I met for a few days and never saw again, beaches, hills, valleys etc. So, I decided to limit myself to five or six pictures for each occasion – and it worked. It meant that I was not throwing them out completely (not quite ready for that) but cut them down dramatically. There were exceptions – family occasions and the like – but not many. And there was*

one holiday that was a disaster so the whole lot went. Aren't we funny – there were some instances with photos so similar that I had to put one behind the other! There are more to go through but I am well on the way."

As always, easy does it. Break down a big shoebox job into smaller projects to accommodate for feelings that might take us by surprise. Limit the task at hand either by number (go through 30 pics) or by project (arrange first part of holiday snaps). Speaking of holiday, should you ever get stressed while packing take a moment to sit down, close your eyes and beam yourself to your destination, right into the adventures ahead. Passport, ticket and credit card are in the bag? Anxiety attacks about leaving the toothbrush behind are optional. Cut the worrying short and put on sunglasses for instant glamour and to entice the sun into putting in an appearance. We are off to scout familiar territory for the unfamiliar as pretend tourists and our traveller alter-ego notices the details we tend to rush past with our commuters' hat on. Permanently at risk of tripping over we are looking upwards, stumbling along like all proper tourists do, as we are not prepared to miss out on a single sight. Especially those that do not officially qualify as such: we admire the guts of audacious greenery that got the better of the asphalt jungle, poking cheeky noses through cracks they have created, successfully reclaiming habitat. The sun has put us on the guest list; we are VIP ticket holders for a private viewing to check out her abstract shadow paintings on the way home. We walk over hundreds of her pristine drawings on the concrete canvas that is the city streets and take in the lightshow and special effects courtesy of a certain fireball.

Photographs are complex symbols. If we lift the veil and peek through their pretence they boil down to bits of paper, code or pixel. They do not qualify for gentle action wash and have to undergo the same rigorous spinning cycle as any other object. The crunch questions remain, "Do you contribute to my overall wellbeing? Are you doing a good job assisting me in enjoying life?" Photographs that have lost their meaning make ideal practice material for letting go. Blurred faces, indescript landscapes, snapshots taken after a few glasses that lose their charm when we have sobered up. Photographs are no exceptions, they resent being a burden to their owners, shoved into boxes or clogging up hard drives. Like any other object or indeed like us, they aspire to make a difference.

Soak up the refreshing energy of current snaps in collages on the fridge, let them save the screen on your phone and laptop or cheer you up peeking out of your purse or wallet. Are pictures showing the entire family or is everybody looking out of their own frame into their own world, turning in opposite directions? Bringing our storyboards up to date helps to emphasise those buds that are about to unfold on the family rose bush. Token gestures in the realm of matter impact positively on history in the making.

Life through a lens, sketch pad in hand we use tools to help us see what we would otherwise cut out. Have you ever taken a picture with your heart? This novelty camera is always ready to shoot and we never have to worry about misplacing or losing it. When we see something beautiful – that might not be remotely pretty – we start scribbling into our inspirations booklet. Key words record the scene in a pictureless and therefore even more evocative snapshot. The handy format makes our camera-cum-album into a companion that can be taken everywhere. Add, read and revel in images arising from the inner eye.

When we temporarily confuse photo-administration issues with proper problems and succumb to being overwhelmed, a glimpse beyond the edge of our nose might be a possible way out. Which percentage of the global population is currently struggling with the unfinished-album-dilemma? Would a stint of volunteering do the trick?

Our world is as big as we want it to be. The light that produces a photograph travels at a speed of 300.000 kilometres per second, racing from earth to moon in just over a second. The light of our sun reaches us within eight minutes. Neighbouring galaxy Andromeda emits rays that hit the blue planet after 2.4 million years. Our galaxy consists of 100 billion planetary systems and is one of 100 billion other galaxies.

V Mental Clutter

Thoughts that take us round in circles

Clearing, like anything else in life, is what you make of it. Comparable to a mud spa treatment for head and heart – messy to start with but ultimately cleansing for body and soul.

> *"I was driving when I suddenly noticed that I wasn't worrying about anything. Instead of thinking about what I had to do, I noticed how the sunlight was streaming through the tree branches."*

Thoughts are powerful creatures. One minute they pose as building blocks for a promising future, the next they turn into free radicals and demolish our world. From our thoughts spring words which turn into deeds and then become habits. Habits form our character which builds destiny.

Occasionally we feel at the mercy of our monkey mind that churns out reasoning and speculation, like a conveyor belt gone mad. Around 60,000 thoughts per day at the last count of statistics, most of them mundane and a whopping 95% exactly the same as yesterday. The scenario of a mind in overdrive has our ears ringing from internal chatter, head throbbing, desperate for any distraction. Hand us the telephone directory anyone, cover to cover it makes for a comparatively entertaining read. Thoughts are powerful enough to lock us into a conceptual prison of our own making but can we fool the guards and clear our way out.

Here is a first-aid tool kit to slow down the thinking merry-go-round. In order to establish what time we live in, we draw a circle that symbolises our thoughts and our mind and divide it into three areas: past, present and future. How much time do we spend – in conversations with others and ourselves – in the ancient world (childhood), middle ages (not too distant past), present and sci-fi future? Do we like the weighting as it is? Could we reshift and zoom ourselves back to the present more often or make space for a few plans, outrageously fabulous ones? When we live in our head, retreating into the past or fast forwarding into the future, we let life slip through our fingers. When we live one day at a time, we get to live all the days of our life.

Phrase junk, data trash, attention grabbing – what gets on our nerves indicates content we could delete from our communications. Constant complaining about trivialities gobbles up energy. No seat on the train? Grumpy colleagues? Oh dear. Injecting questions, "What would you rather do, what have you always been dreaming about?" steers the tirade into more promising waters. Classifying something as a problem is almost like casting it in concrete, as all our energy goes into What-Is. How about remodelling the problem into a challenge? *I should* gets an overhaul, passes the MOT with flying colours and comes back as *I could* – have another go at the paper work. Everything we think or say is an affirmation. How many of our 16,000 words a day are a positive force? What do we really *have* to do? When we pay attention to our words and thoughts we make out self-inflicted constraints and upgrade to moaning 2.0, where we no longer moan because we are miserable, but because it makes us happy.

Gossip signals that there is not enough going on in our own life that is worth talking about, so we resort to casually dropping the odd condescending remark to keep self-doubt in check. Those who know about their own greatness let others keep theirs. Let's be utterly great and keep track of "Who benefits if I say this out loud?"

Thoughts and conversations are carriers of vibes that either pull us up, kick-start something inside or leave us washed out. What can we hear when sitting down by the banks of our own stream of consciousness? Which thoughts hold us back, which ones catapult us onto the path that has *headway* written all over it?

If we tune into our mind and pick up arguments with people on the other side of the globe, the office or the sofa, we change station and focus our attention on a self-created instant mantra. Repeat an uplifting word – joy, peace, sun – until there is music in the air. Thoughts are closely connected to the vibration of life energy. Pull a favourite poem or prayer out of a notebook or memory bank to counteract the white noise of a mind in overdrive. Dive into the calming vibes; dissolve tormenting thoughts, eyes wide shut.

A note-taking device, an old fashioned pen will do, kept next to the bed serves as a tool to switch off incessantly blinking warning lights of *don't forget to..*! When we are thinking – talking to ourselves – tongue and lower jaw are tensed up. We can slow down internal chatter by consciously relaxing them. Then we can make out again the remote sounds that were drowned out by internal buzzing. Relaxed shoulders, head slowly circling we plug ourselves back in to the crescendo of life around us: clocks ticking, hearts beating, wood creaking, the buzzing singsong of the fridge switching itself on and off, flurries of wind whispering sweet nothings. The soundtrack of life itself makes us move out of our head back into where we happen to be sitting, standing, walking – travelling the world by going down the road.

Tune into a body part to wind down, divert consciousness inwards and listen to the gentle throbs of life pulsating through you. Welcome to inner space. What do lips feel like from the inside, can you discern your forehead or little toe? Thoughts are drifting in and out without being tied down by assessment. There is no need to run after life. If we become still, very still, it comes to us. Meditation is not about techniques that only reveals themselves to the devoted after years of instructions on how to produce strange guttural sounds while knotting the body in the one correct way, to end up sitting there thinking, "Come on inner peace I haven't got all day." If you cannot see yourself joining the ohm-brigades, simply click yourself back into the now for some meditation to go. It is a state of being attentive even while running for the bus or stuffing dirty laundry into the machine. Meditation is about calming down on the inside, no matter what is going on in the surround sound action flick we are starring in. It is about interrupting the movie in our head to zoom ourselves back onto the road we are cycling on. Shifting out of automatic into an awareness of how we are here. Pulling weeds, chopping veg, fixing a gadget, arranging flowers – you know best what makes you forget about clock time. Meditation is to handle objects consciously, reconnecting to sensuality and contemplation. Meditation is about discovering what has been there all along. It is seeing rainbows in soap bubbles while doing the dishes. Taking a closer look at a face, at the leaf that comes gently tumbling down to be swept up again by a gusty cough of wind.

Meditation is sitting on the dock of the bay, wasting time. Falling in love with silence, listening to its spell. Taking a stroll around our favourite castle in the air. Enjoying moments free from wanting or waiting. Reflecting back the light, quiet like the sun-sparkling surface of a pond, dazzling with diamond droplets.

Time management – the end of a myth

Physicists do not believe in time and mystics nod their heads in agreement, smiling wisely. The rest of us have to carry on carrying on; squeezed in between alarms going off and paradoxes playing out around us: an afternoon is stretching itself out into eternity while another year has whizzed past in no time.

How could you possibly 'manage' this slippery, unpredictable something that keeps running through your fingers at the speed of light? Time management is a myth. Of course we still sit up and take notice at the presentation of yet another 'latest technique' because it all boils down to energy management and vitality is a resource we can never get enough of.

A professor fills a jar with stones and looks up, "Is this full now?" Nodding of heads all round. She proceeds to put pebbles in between the rocks, same question, feedback more hesitant. The third step has sand trickling into the in remaining gaps. The jar symbolises a day of our life and the grains of sand are the chores; the eternal mantra of, "I just quickly have to do/clean/wash/sort/finish that." The rocks stand for inner priorities and if we do not stay on high alert, our days will be filling up with sand one after another. Outcome: colourful bucket and spade to dig up some breathing space for the rocks – diary clearout here we come. Any 'used to be fun'spare time activity that has turned the corner from pleasure to pain has to go; we reorganise our life around priorities of our own making. (In case you feel tempted to throw in the all time favourite, "*Yes, but,*" don't. Not yet. Pretty please.) Time management means creating a balance that works for us, to find out what we need. Helpful habits are to refrain from doing something just because everybody else does it and to refrain from doing something just because everybody else thinks we should do it.

Be brave enough to end a telephone conversation or meeting when the fizz has gone. As soon as we notice a 'wanna get out of here' feeling, the communication exercise is energy sapping for everybody involved.

Time limits are helpful because they create structure and focus. Make up a deadline instead of embarking on a project with the intention of carrying on 'until it is finished' or the cows come home. Next step towards the pastures green of feeling on top of whatever appointment life throws at us: reminders and to-do-lists are scribbled straight into the diary. This approach cuts down on bits of paper cruising in and out of our life and conveniently doubles as a reality check: is it possible to squeeze four 90 minute tasks into one morning?

Time out, indulging in procrastination or social media are promoted to being official members of the schedule. Tasks that have never been taken into account now get proper diary entries and allocated time slots. 1pm to 2pm: dawdling, daydreaming, hatching holiday plans. 8pm to 8am: switch off, twitter off, everything wired and networked remains deprived of juice. The working day regains a definite end and we regain a clear head. One out of three (morning, afternoon, evening) has no work-related phone calls or messages creeping in. There is a life waiting out there, offline. All yours. Go get it.

Next up for a clearout is the endless list with expectations towards ourselves. Do skills and ambitions match? As Einstein said, everybody is a genius, but if you judge fish by their ability to ride a bike or climb a tree they end up feeling stupid all their life. We are gifted but it is our job to open the package.

Race horses gallop to their hearts' content, a tortoise is hard-wired to a different pace. Both reach their goals because they honour their unique speed limits. If we are carved from slow-motion, life in the fast lane is not our idea of fun. Instead we learn to stand like a tree and take in ivy's demonstration of how to surpass yourself slowly. Pace does not know better or worse; why force ourselves into a rhythm that is not ours by nature? When about to get stuck in a clearing session we take a break or stop. Some are doers, ninja-busting action heroes who only feel alive when they have a minimum of seven projects on the go at once. Others are in love with process and conservation; at home in contemplation and tranquillity. We need both. Let's be brave and live the pace that feels right for us, whatever it may be today: rocket ship or rocking chair.

In the story of the woodcutters one man is beavering away without a pause, the other one takes a break every now and again to disappear behind the hut. At the end of the day the pieceworker has felled 25 trees whereas the more laid-back lumberjack achieved a result of 30. The guy who had hacked away as if trying to smash the sound barrier asks what his colleague had been up to at break time. "I sharpened my tools."

Making time to look after ourselves and recharge physically, mentally, emotionally or spiritually pays off. Exercising, studying, relaxing, reconnecting – which of our tools are due an overhaul?

Sometimes we feel whacked even before we have poked a toe out of the covers, crawling back under to get away from the alarm. One of those days that wallop us before they have even started; where we do not feel up to what seems like a triathlon of obligations awaiting us, finishing line nowhere to be seen. Sometimes the only means of transport available is a leap of faith. Even stress has its upsides. Adopting a 'busyaholic' or martyr role makes us feel needed and better than others which becomes an auxiliary drive belt that keeps us going. Stress also comes in handy to bypass responsibility or delay decisions. We can punish others or get attention: look-at-me-everyone, slaving away again. For you.

Perhaps we only allow ourselves to rest or to look after our own needs after we have gone over the limit, only stop working and functioning when we get ill. Society has sanctioned physical discomfort as a way towards getting some peace and quiet. Ringing in to tell boss, colleagues or clients, "Sorry, I somehow don't feel up to it today, everything seems a bit too much at the moment, I think I need a rest," is not an option. Waving about a doctor's certificate stating the official breakdown of body components ticks the right boxes. Bouts of migraine qualify as an accepted problem set, bouts of being overwhelmed do not. Subtle blockages take a while to manifest into physical symptoms.

If we are feeling blue, we could try to paint ourselves a different colour or start dancing in the rain while waiting for the storm to pass? We could stop giving ourselves a hard time and start to have a go at stress instead: starve it. Change our diet and heap invigorating helpings of laughter and zest for life on the plate we had misplaced amongst the must-dos. Which daft idea is powerful enough to get us out of self-inflicted routine lows? When nothing goes right, go left – spontaneous miniature crazinesses, here we come. A night walk with no light source but silvery moonshine. Hopping on a random bus to find out what is going on beyond the last stop. Picking up litter in the park, blissfully unworried about what others might think. Open the front door and step out, right into the great outdoors. Invite aliens over for a cup of coffee after we have overheard them asking, "Do you believe in humans?" to discuss their pet subject, life on planet earth. "Tell us, what is it like to get into the guts of the pyramids, into a cave or an igloo? Have you ever jumped off a cliff into a smooth layer of sea underneath, holding your breath until you hit the water? Have you had ocean waves come towards you, screaming with excitement until they crash over your head?" And then we have to smile apologetically and say, "Sorry no, not really. But I could tell you everything about television programmes and facebook updates, decades worth!" At age 60 we have spent an average 15 of those years glued to screens. The contemporary mod cons, 'Comfort & Co', are dangerous companions. First they distract us, then they put us to sleep. What would we rather do: keep consuming the ideas of others, or have a go at manifesting our own? This day is a one off. It will never come back.

So called 'time management' is about learning what is running us, setting priorities and balancing our life by following our own rhythm. It is about keeping track of expectations and managing our attitude as we organise a busy life. Take your pick – today, I will be: unflappable. Ready to laugh. Giddy with joy. In awe of the wonder of life. Kind to (almost) everyone I meet. Giggling about things that are *not* funny. Open to adventure.

We owe it to the gift of life to live our best life.

Putting off procrastination – once and for all!

If we do not deal with things, they end up dealing with us. Often we spend more time thinking about doing something than it actually takes to do it. "I'll wipe that down, give X a call, put up the picture, dust this, mend that." Two minutes worth of action, the thought pursued to infinity. Psychological reasons for procrastination can be a fear of failure or an act of rebellion: getting our own back on the ever-present inner adult with a dose of refreshing anarchy. When we let the to-dos drift off towards the horizon we trip ourselves up as this homemade stress undermines our health. Fortunately there is an instant cure available: as soon as we have tied up the first one of those loose ends, we feel invigorated. Give it a try and see how good it feels to get it done – send the text message, post the letter, fill in the form – there and then. Elaborate collections of procrastination beauties gnaw away at us until we make it a habit to do anything that takes less than two minutes straight away: exchange numbers, clean the sink, write it down, take it upstairs. Why should to-do-lists consist of cheesy duties only? We devise an alternative version that includes as many charmers: explode the lungs with deep intake of crisp morning air. Go for walks whenever we feel like it, no lunch break, dog or other official get-out clause required. Let radiant, soul-warming colour schemes move into wardrobe and office spaces. Laugh out loud if we want to, cry if we have to, even while negotiating an inner city jungle with its faces that might stop and stare. Or smile, and pass a tissue.

Habits are spider webs that turn into wires over time, often too small to be felt until they are too strong to be broken. They are good at getting us stuck in an attitude that takes everything for granted and the lifeless dread that comes with being a stowaway in your own life. Crosscheck: take ten minutes to come up with the ultimate bullet point collection, the list to end all lists. Everything that is roaming around in the vastness of our mind's wild wild West gets pinned down. The mother of lists is being treated with exquisite finishing touches: oversized squares after every task, ready for the feel-good 'done!' reward tick. In order to make sure that the ticks do not end up as an endangered species, even the tiniest to-do gets to stand alone. Wanted: sew on button, change light bulb, reply to email, send off card. All of the miniature tasks on the run will now have a hard time outsmarting us and not get away unticked. Mammoth tasks cannot get a seat at the list table; complexities are broken down into bitsized 'managable-ness'. Now take a moment to look down on your listed work of art – its crisp clarity is a tonic in itself.

Next step is to transfer selected points over into the diary and remaining to-dos are either: being dealt with (now), being delegated (to whom, when), done by (deadline) or dropped from the list altogether (crossed out). Surely you agree that the ensuing delight is comparable to the effects of a long weekend by the beach. Who would want to bake cookies or go online if they now have the most superior procrastination project of all at their disposal – the decluttering of another drawer!

As we have done so well, we spoil ourselves rotten and indulge in a favourite activity. "Easier said than done," remote grumbling noises; "I love surfing, how do I fit that in between supper preparation and doing the dishes?" When is the next day off, how can we create one? Who will look after the kids, pets and pot plants? Off we go, planning, arranging, reshuffling, making things happen; looking forward to an adventure of our own making.

"Right now off to Brussels and Strasbourg on a one week study trip on my own. Why? Because I wanted to do this forty years ago – and didn't have the courage. One friend said, if I don't tell anyone, maybe they won't notice I'm not 17 anymore. Isn't that good!"

No more putting off, pulling it off is the name of the game.

Multi-tasking – the end of another myth

Doing four things at once does not work; it never has and never will. Even if we give it fancy Latin names and keep trying regardless. 'Multi-tasking' is a myth and the time has come to name names and call it a day. If we concentrate on one thing only we achieve so much more. Why would anyone want to plug in the iron while booting up the computer, switching on the oven, answering the phone and starting to write a card? First we lose sight of what comes next then we lose 'it' altogether. If we begin the next task only after having finished the one at hand, we enjoy 100% of the satisfaction that comes with having accomplished something.

How does this sound, only one document at a time gets to reside on the desk? Once dealt with, it moves on into its file home or gets recycled. In case that sounds slightly utopian, it can still serve as inspiration to stop unnecessary 'multi-tasking' and reintroduce focus back into our communications. We can think three times faster than we speak which means we are busy constructing a reply while the other person is still talking. Far from being all ears we are drafting answers, lying in wait for a chance to break in. True listening is quiet concentration that allows for accessing the message beyond the words. Is this addressed to heart or intellect?

As the saying goes – before enlightenment: cutting wood and carrying water; after enlightenment: cutting wood and carrying water. The washing and the washing up will never go away, maintenance is here to stay and best described as the exact opposite of breathtaking. The only thing we can change (apart from instantly refraining from ever ironing T-shirts or towels again) is our attitude towards these tasks. Do what has to be done and transform chores into love made visible. Conscious cleaning is clearing and as magical when combined with intention. We anchor higher energy in the room while vacuuming; ask for clarity regarding the next step forward when we clean the windows. Organised, light-flooded surroundings enhance the energy flow which reduces stress. Even dusting makes sense in the decluttering universe. Cooking as a mixing of magical potions, stirring infusions of tenderness for those about to enjoy our meal.

All is full of love.

Electronic clutter

One broadsheet newspaper contains roughly the amount of information that a person alive in medieval times would have taken in over a lifetime. Information on just about everything has become so vast as to be nearly unmanageable. The latest statistics say that more data is now being created in every 48-hour period than in the past 30,000 years put together. Wi-fi is everywhere, technology has invaded our life and chains us to the virtual office 24/7. The whole world is after us, always – stop. Only if we cannot recall where the off button is hiding on this latest Smartphone and how to work it. Time off, weekend, how do you spell that? Apparently, "I wish I hadn't worked so hard" features in the top four of major regrets of the dying.

Social media got us hooked on the next status update, comment, retweet, somehow-acknowledge-me fix. We send a message, publish a post and expect instant reactions. Come on you global followers, and pronto. Snapping out of it is an option as are time limits for catching up on the permanent updates of facebook & Co. We drag ourselves away from double-checking and switch back from virtual reality into the 3D version of it. Grow roots, touch base and have the lunch break meander gently into the afternoon. Life is not lived in the glow of a monitor. Being glued to a screen never beats being glued to another human. We take a break from flickering and stare at life instead, let our eyes wander until they find something they want to rest on. Something as unreal as a tree. Some of them can fly, we glimpse them whooshing past train windows and windscreens. We stay wide awake, determined not to miss half an ounce of this life that is being shovelled towards us on escalators floating up while we go underground. On the train we look up to see how life is pushing its way towards us, squashing in through subway doors that have just slid open. Snapping shut again we are in it together, sharing what oxygen is left in the carriage, riding towards the next stop.

Tapping the off button has become an essential skill. Information is now so rapid it causes a state of constant interrupt which affects cognition and deeper thinking. Concentration comes back when we stop jumping between online temptations and projects we have to get on with. We restructure the workflow by grouping similar tasks together: return phone calls, deal with emails, then a stint of invoicing. Redundant newsletters or blog subscriptions are cancelled; failing that, redirected into junk mail folders. All radical, we cut down on news consumption and go on an information-detox. We make peace with the fact that we cannot always be in the know, up-to-date, kept in the loop.

Arranging meetings via typing or texting can be momentarily less of an energy expense than talking, but it can take umpteen messages until something has been agreed. Emailing is not an option when one phone call replaces about ten mails. We resist the temptation of the CC button even at the cost of depriving the boss and colleagues from getting insights into our riveting and groundbreaking email interactions.

We fondly call it research, but clicking our way around the net could mean we are just not ready for the real thing yet. Instead of surfing for hours on end – there might be a better deal out there, somewhere – let's be brave and brief and put our name down for the class. Arrange the long overdue medical appointment, boiler servicing, garden clean up. Book the tickets, the table, the long weekend. Nailed it, bang. Hip hip hurray!

In an ideal world we reply to an email at the first opening click. In the real world it can take a few more. Here is a vision: open and read it and either reply straight away or make use of the wonderful feature that is the delete button – completion with the sweet sound of success 'click'. On our way towards the thrilling prospect of an empty inbox we are bumping into fear again, wafting about with its threats, so vague and so well known. "Better hold on to that, probably best to print it as well, twice. Photocopying wouldn't do any harm either. You never…" Getting rid of the electronic ballast is as much of a relief as clearing the decks on the three-dimensional stage. Unblocking on the outside always instigates a parallel process on the inside and welcomes us into the bliss of free-flowing energy. Living in peace and harmony with our 'keyboarded' counterparts can be done when we let computers do the things that they are good at, like remembering everything with great accuracy. Meanwhile us humans get to do the things that we are good at: fun, intuition, emotion, creativity, friends and family.

Next on the agenda: the freefall into nothingness. Cut the umbilical cord to the Smartphone. Chances are – unlikely as it may seem – we will survive up to two hours without updates. Umbrella, tissues, lip balm, workload, the must-read and all other 'can't-do-withouts' are being grounded as well and have to stay home to keep the phone company. We are setting off without the slightest trace of a bag, drifting out into the evening air like a tiny white feather. We take the wind by the hand and are blown upwards. Safely landed on our feet again, we tilt the head skywards, getting tipsy from raindrops bursting on our lips, gulping down mouthfuls of wind for afters. We watch twilight fading out the colours, getting out her liner to present us with nothing but clear-cut outlines. Leaving us bright-eyed and perception-enhanced; overflowing with gorgeous bubbly on the inside. This preciously fleeting feeling of *being alive*.

VI Emotional Clutter

Did you ever walk through a park, listen to a concert, hug a child – and nothing seemed to get through? We do not always have direct access to our five basic emotions love, anger, grief, fear and jealousy. These natural feelings are like emotional start ramps into a fulfilled life. When they are suppressed they reverse roles from life-affirming to life-negating. If anger is not lived as a spontaneous no-thanks-indicator, it mutates into aggression or hatred. Grief helps us cope with change, loss and death. Unfaced or unexpressed, it transforms into feeling sorry for ourselves, constant complaining and overall bitterness. Life-saving fear becomes life-negating fear and jealousy, originally conceived as a motivating force, ends in drama. Clearing allows for one-on-one encounters with our natural emotions at a gentle pace. Clutter marks the playing field where we experiment with immediate feeling-feedback. We practice dealing with complex emotions in a boxed-up safe zone, approaching the Big Five, let them come through and then up. As soon as it gets overwhelming we can pull the brakes and put the lid back on. Tomorrow is another day.

Feelings about ourselves are directly related to our surroundings which is why picking up stuff from the floor, prettifying or fixing something is such a great idea when we are after an instant lift.

Now that we have become seasoned pros when it comes to dealing with objects, we can move on to test run various moods. We have established what was weighing down on our shelves – what is weighing down on our heart?

Pointless feelings

Are you ready to jump onto the rollercoaster that is the courage to express feelings? Hooting with joy, taking the odd shouting match in your stride if need be. If raised voices or eyebrows would cramp your style there is the option of polite moderation and, "Fine, thanks." Emotions leave energetic footprints that remain as vibrations in us and in the things we surround ourselves with. If an object is contaminated with bitter feelings, someone else can live with it more happily as they are not burdened by those negative associations.

Which ones are the clutter feelings that are draining and make us run on the spot? Coming in at number one, worrying can claim pride of place in the gallery of pointless feelings. It gobbles up life-force without changing anything for the better. We still like to engage in that mind game as it provides us with an illusion of control in an open-ended situation. As long as we keep ourselves busy worrying, we feel as if we are 'preparing' for all eventualities and are therefore no longer at the mercy of not-knowing. This explains why this pseudo-action is quite a popular past time. However, pondering the fact that we attract what we focus on might help to break the habit and make brainstorming solutions a more attractive option than going for another 'worry-up'. When we stress ourselves out because we are trying to control an uncertain outcome or the future at large, the 'worry-buster-question' can work wonders. Sit down and ask yourself, "What major problem have I got right *now*, while sitting here sipping a cup of tea?"

Dwelling on guilt and regret can be a refusal to move on. We are branding ourselves as bad instead of human, having fondly entertained the idea of being the one exception to the rule – but hey, nobody is perfect. Learn the lesson, ideally avoid repeating it in exactly the same way tomorrow and off to brand new, even more exciting blunders. A ritual might help to move on, like writing the sticky issue on a note and creating a miniature ceremony around letting go of it. We could set the paper alight, bury it, or literally close that chapter by shutting it in somewhere. Keep experimenting until you find a format that makes sense to you and feels right.

Forgiving is not about having another go at getting our lovely halo back after all. It is about letting go of our share of the hurt, as a present to ourselves. Half of any grumpy energies we fabricate keep hanging around, sticking to us. What we do to others, we do to ourselves. Buddha compared holding anger to drinking poison and expecting the other person to die. We do not have to forgive an act that was unforgivable, but we can make peace with the person. We set ourselves free when we no longer revolve around our own issues.

When animals clash, they leave it at that. Humans like it more complicated and remain masters of the universe when it comes to headache fabrication. They can carry on going over an incident in their mind for days on end; months of playing the same slightly insane track on repeat (we can take producer credits after all!) "I can't believe she/he did that to me. That's it. I've had enough. Who do they think they are? I'll give them a piece of my mind. That's outrageous! You wait. I can't believe she/he did that to me.

That's it. I've had enough. Who do they think they..." Next time round we will not get stuck but be wise as ducks, flap our wings to shake the anger out with the water, let bygones be bygones and flutter on to the most promising looking patch of grass further up the pond. Alternatively, we will treat ourselves to screaming into a pillow, whacking a mattress or taking it out on that dusty rug that was in dire need of a good whopping all along.

When we love ourselves enough, forgiving becomes irrelevant. Everyone always does their best. The other party feels just as right, otherwise the argument would not have come up. How about another sideway glance into the proverbial mirror? What can we make out this time round? Are we ready to quit projecting our strengths and weaknesses onto others to keep them as our own? Take a step back, "What have I contributed to this situation?" When nothing else works try something adventurous: communicate. Starting sentences with *I* instead of *you* takes the edge off and can get a dialogue stuck on the rocks off the ground again. "You don't get it, do you? What's new," sounds slightly different from, "I feel hurt."

Have fun with the disassociation technique; step out of the situation and look down at the scene from another angle. Imagine it as part of a soap opera or in cartoon format. Will this remark still be upsetting ten years from now?

Inner resistance is like barbed wire that keeps us prisoner of a situation as it energises unwanted circumstances and therefore reinforces them. Frantic endeavour hinders more than it helps. 'Trying too hard-mode' wears us out with little to show. Change course, quit resisting the unwanted and be all *for* something instead.

Throw your weight behind a positive and get into the flow by patiently accepting what is while pursuing a vision.

As long as we insist on being right we make someone else wrong. We do not have to attend every argument we are invited to. An aggressive remark is like a letter; if we refuse to accept it, it is being returned to sender. When negative energy is pointed towards us we can sidestep it and let it whoosh past. Only if it hits a sounding board within us, will we take the bait and let the drama unfold. We accept an accusation the moment we start to get defensive or justify ourselves. If we deal with differences or clashes in relationships in a conscious and proactive manner they are inspiring sources of growth.

It is not about what others are doing or not doing, it is about how we choose to react. Being the critic is easy; walking the talk of a different way of being is not. Let's see how far we get in a role reversal, just for a few hours. How long can we keep up meaning what we say and saying what we mean? Follow in Gandhi's footsteps and practice harmlessness, not hurting ourselves, others or the planet, being the change we want to see in the world?

Emotions are signposts, volunteering their directions – *don't go there, try this way*. Prolonged episodes of feeling trapped, bored, disappointed or unworthy are as draining as permanently grappling with pessimism or impatience, succumbing to chronic doubt, anger or self-righteousness. Emotions are connected to our attitude and change with it. Sometimes we prefer to deal with 'family-ar' trouble, sticking to a pain we know rather than crawling out of our comfort zone. Suffering can be easier than breaking free.

Unaware that they have stopped being of assistance years ago, we are dragging decades-worth of ingrained patterns with us. These sets of behaviour may have served as life savers in childhood; they were the crutches that got us through the day. Hauled over into adulthood they make us repeat scenarios, hopeful they might end happily ever after twenty-second time round. Suffering is *not* good for the soul. Its value is in showing us how to stop suffering.

When the inner critics sneak back into our thoughts we are adamant. "Thanks for making me aware of my shortcomings yet again but I think I've heard that one before. Your services are no longer required; may I advise early retirement or show you to the door?" And then, smiling pleasantly, we boot them out. They will be back in no time, of course. When we accept that they stop by every now and again, we are not upset when they show up, their best pals the inner judges in tow who adore their fulltime job of, well, judging. "Oh hi, you again." We are not making it a duel 'me against negative thoughts' and stay at ease with the comings and goings of judgement and despair. We no longer try to banish the critical voices from our head but say, "Thanks for your views," and they feel heard. End of discussion.

Relationships that have gone 'baggy' cannot be disposed of at the recycling bank but habitual loyalty qualifies as much for a clearout as any spare rain coat. Friendships that live up to their name energise us; they keep us alive on the inside. How do we feel when thinking of meeting a particular friend? There are billions of people on this planet and it is up to us who we spend time with. 'Helper syndrome' can be decluttered with the realisation that saving someone else is impossible. We can try to crack jokes to cheer up a depressed person, an effort that will not make up for underlying energy deficits. Tugging with the best of intentions, we cannot pull someone off their path onto a route that is not theirs to go. Everyone is on a journey. We are never responsible for the happiness of another but always for our own. Let's get tanked up with morning dew, with the gleaming glare of city lights. Wade fearlessly into the red-rustling sea of leaves that autumn has washed up against our feet. Watch the flaming orange circle set the horizon on fire.

Flying into a rage that does not harm anyone else is a fantastic energy source, a seat on a rocket to the stars. An infuriated, "That remains to be seen!" roar lights a bonfire under our comfy chair, makes us jump up and leave what we cannot stand any longer to go after what we want.

Envy makes for a brilliant motivational tool. It shows us what we would like to achieve or do, who or where we would like to be. What is the first step towards being the person we want to be?

Boredom is the messenger of fascinating news. Is it time to move on? Where to? Nobody wins if we keep running on the spot, denying our gifts. As soon as we start to live up to our talents, the world is growing through and with us. Being happy and fulfilled is the greatest present we can give to others.

Affirmations are phrases used to reprogramme thought processes. We are perfectly entitled to reiterate what we are not good at and hire a permanent parking space in this perception and therefore reality. Who decides what goes on in our head? When we catch ourselves reeling off alleged shortcomings – full stop. Add another dot and a half circle and end up with a smiley and a new version of the story. Failure no longer trips us up, but spurs us on.

Affirmations are not meant to be applied as local anaesthetics. It makes little sense to reel off, "I am in peace," while barking mad because our effort to repress feelings ties up energy. The big bad wolf of darker feeling tones will not swallow us whole, but the waves of emotions make for great surfing: see it coming towards us, let ourselves be carried up and down and then up again, ride it out. "What is this moment trying to tell me?" Become aware of the feeling, work through it, move on. One of the most straightforward and powerful forms of therapy is to feel an emotion the moment it shows up. To not push it back down when it comes knocking, not analyzing it, but feeling it. Then it is most likely to disappear without leaving scars. Clearing can teach us to stop ignoring or tolerating pain and to grieve for the hurts in life when they happen instead of making our heart heavy by lugging them around. The best way out is through.

The boss from hell inspired one client to hand in his notice which eventually led to the career change he had been dreaming about. Without the assistance of this obnoxious helper he might have put it off forever. With hindsight experiences verging on the limit of what is bearable often gift us value. Like in old school photography, we use the negatives to develop.

Think of someone who is or was an adversary (it could also be an illness or a traumatic experience), then choose a person or incident that had a positive impact on your life. What are/were their roles: catalyst, messenger, challenger, midwife? Soul mate, angel, teacher? What else could we think of? These people and events came into our life as an incentive for change, fast forwarding our development. Again we have to pack away the 'Good / Bad' labels before we get to stick them on.

After a stroke of fate we can stop at the question, "Why me? ", or allow pain to transform us and eventually inspire us to ask, "Why not me?" Why should everybody else have to deal with stormy waters while we are entitled to a life like a never-ending cruise, infinite buffet and sunshine included? Everything can be taken away from us, but the most profound human freedom is to choose our attitude whatever situation we find ourselves in, said Viktor Frankl. Heaviness lifts when we rephrase, "I have to," into "I choose to," the lightness seeping through from the language into inner and outer worlds.

We cannot change our whole life. We can only approach the task ahead in a way we have not tried before. We may not be able to improve a relationship, but we can think about the next interaction. We cannot alter the past or control the future but we are in charge of what we are doing right now.

We cannot change everything. We can only change one, small thing – and that's all it takes.

Patent remedies

Creating our own sets of beliefs is more empowering than adopting ready-mades. What is this season's must-have for us? We all swing to our own rhythm, inhabiting individual paradigms. What does crisis mean to us? A spiritual experience of endings and new beginnings? Only if we insist on defining failure as such, does it get to blow itself up into one. Otherwise it remains an experience and an opportunity to start over. The end of a relationship is the beginning of a new chapter of happiness for everybody involved. How do we define bliss? Hours in the shower? Toes in the sand? A day without a timetable? Is success the high flying job, family of four, owning more than others? How about a funkier offering, where we describe success as no longer being a victim of our mood swings, as having overcome conditioned reactions, got out of rehashing dramas.

Distracted by the silent noise of things, we are in danger of settling for too little love or joy or community. When did we last access our true identity and to feel it in our bones that we *are* a gift to the world?

Top three ways of behaving that throw a spanner in the works of our personal development are the refusal to accept help, finding excuses why something is not working or ignoring information or advice because it does not conform to our views.

Let's treat ourselves to soul searching-time. "What do I want at this point, what do I think I *should* want? What are soul priorities, what are head priorities?" We can fly as high as the dreams we dare to live as soon as we get out of the Either-Or Club and unsubscribe from its mantra 'who wants to be happy if they can be normal'. Members are convinced that you have to make a choice of either earning good money or doing what you love. The most commonly available myth describes life as a classroom where outward achievement is being graded as the be-all and end-all. Another popular offering is the school of thought that life is erratic so we had better get to a safe place and stay put for the next 25 years. Luckily life has not been patented as a lame compromise – what does your motto sound like? Life is for living, our ticket to join the And-And Club. As a revolutionary founding member we dump the dustiest thought patterns and put up novel ones instead. Exhibit number one: life is a gift. Every morning we get to unwrap a new day out of the sunrise it comes in. Mere existing, getting by and muddling along are sold out. Up for grabs – take one, get one free – pleasure sampling, cheekiness collecting, panting for air, jumping for joy, paddling in stormy waters, somersaults galore.

We can get irate about the fact that the train is ten minutes late again or be deliriously happy when it shows up in the end. Because elsewhere on the planet we would climb onto the roof of a bus that turns up once a day to take the spare seat next to the chickens. Shifting gears from autopilot into appreciation mode is excellent news for our immune system and more invigorating than an energy drink. Joy is like a vegetable, it can be cultivated. Would you like to start an appreciation diary or simply count down what opened your heart, freehand, just before drifting off into sleep? For how long can we keep them open, the eyes of our soul, before reverting back into not-noticing mode? The world needs our laughing lips and lopsided views to throw it back into a balance off the beaten tracks.

We have the option to lock ourselves into an alarmed pseudo-security or reinvent ourselves every so often. Any moment could be the potential gateway to file away certificates and start over, turning personal strengths into the next unheard of profession, making up the job description as we go along to join podcasters and bloggers in their untraditional trades.

We prescribe ourselves regular clearouts as preventative measures against symptoms of numbing; sip from the magic potion that is cultivating a curiosity of the known and take another look at what we got used to getting used to. Is it any wonder? Yes it is. Chat to our alien friend about a 'typical' day. "I get on a train (what is that?) and go into town (which is?) The soul feeds on the tiniest gestures of goodwill on our part. Try smiles instead of frowning whilst sitting in front of a screen, the face mirrors back inwards the emotions it shows to the world. Reconnect to the fuse box of sensual delights where the living is easy, where stars and sun keep on shining. For us. They do, no matter what.

Every now and again it is worth trying to take more pronounced measures to snap out of habitually cutting out the sublime spectacles we are surrounded by. Reminding ourselves how many things we take for granted that could be gone by tonight. Pretend we have just received the diagnosis that we are going to lose our eyesight, or imagine an accident that would cut us off from the luxuries of being able to move unaided. Come back from this mind game and fly around on these miraculous walking sticks that have been conveniently attached so we can go places. Imagine, there would be no *next time* to devalue what is happening right now: this is the last piece of ice cold melon, juices running, fingers dripping, tongue curling in delight.

Would you rather pitch your tent in a feeling of being hemmed in or start colouring in outside the lines? When did you last have a shower outside, fully clothed, rain drumming on your head, slowly seeping through the fabric, running down over your face, making eyelashes drip and eyes water with tears of joy brought to you by the heavens? Wind ruffling our hair, trying a blow-dry to make up for the soak while we are looking at this latest silent movie, now showing in the drive-in cinema near you on that grey, white, blue, black, silvery, golden screen we call sky. Walk off into the lands out of the blue with our thunderstorm hairdo, trusting that events we did not plan for are spiritual pointers.

VII Staying afloat

The art of not-buying

When you are multi-passionate it can get hairy fast on the shopping front. 'Fashionistas', craft lovers or DIY-pundits will find it impossible to come across anything they could not use, keep, barter or bid for. Human society is consuming 30% more material than is sustainable from the world's resources. Humanity, as in those 85 countries currently exceeding their domestic bio-capacities, are compensating for their lack of raw materials by depleting the stocks of others. Consumer culture encourages us to want ever more; the first credit card was introduced in 1972 to 'take the waiting out of the wanting'. Social psychologists believe that the manic consumerism of today is partly rooted in the information age. Humans are hardwired to want what others have. Our parents tried to keep up with the neighbours; we are trying to keep up with our global average of 450 facebook friends. The paradigm has shifted. Or has it? Life is not about our friend count, it is still about the friends we can count on.

So we just bravely got rid of (what felt like) half of our life – and a few weeks later everything has filled up again. Blink and you miss it. Life is like a shopping mall, only once we start looking around do we realise how many things we have to do without. How did we manage to get this far without those virtually dust-free, responsibly sourced, stainless steel, state-of-the-art, handcrafted, easy to apply, collapsible, reversible, inflatable – bare necessities?

How do we prevent stuff from sneaking back in behind our back? Getting used to reclaimed space takes time, the new emptiness feels scary to begin with which is why we might resort to filling it up again. Not by proactively *doing* anything of course. We just sit there, minding our own business, read a paper and then pick up the odd bargain on the way home. We have to be patient with ourselves, but also ask potential fellow occupants to sit for a brief interview. "Please answer the following two questions if you want to move in with me: do I need you? Do I love you?" If the object has come through with double yeses, there is still a helpful golden rule to bear in mind: when something new comes in, something old has to leave. Occasionally we do things we do not enjoy in order to purchase things we do not need. Let's face it, deep down we have remained the hunter gatherers we started out as a few millennia ago, carrying bones, berries and mushrooms back home to the cave. Today it is still the odd bone, berry or mushroom and then some multipacks and special offers and other everyday essentials we happened to come across.

Clutter is not choosy as to who it moves in with. The phenomenon does not just apply to obviously congested homes; all of us have amassed too much stuff. It is not about the amount of clutter but about the awareness of how it affects us. Organised clutter lovers take pride in neatly labelling their surplus possessions, deriving exquisite pleasure from dreaming up clever storage ideas for stuff they never use. Here is another inspiring real life story from a clearing class member who had been looking around for an umbrella stand. Until, one fine day, it dawned on her, *"Why was I searching for a stand? What made me think I had to buy another item to store umbrellas that I didn't like or use anyway? I didn't need one in the first place! Two thirds of the umbrellas I owned were ghastly or broken or too big – or all of the above – so why keep them?!"* She decided to get rid of the brollies knocking around the hallway (quite literally, as they had the annoying habit of falling over with a loud thump). Now the unwanted umbrellas have found new homes and her home feels like new with free-flowing energy in the hallway. This story is an example of how we do not see the wood for the trees; kidding ourselves into hunting for storage when we could let go of the items instead.

When do we buy? Are we getting a few things to take our mind off a few other things? What are we after when embarking on a shopping spree: inner peace? A sense of belonging, or feeling good about ourselves? Are we buying into an image? Are feelings of security on the list, or are we trying to purchase attention or admiration? All of the above – in short: happiness?

A story tells of a tourist strolling around the harbour when he spots a local fisherman dozing on his boat, soaking up the sun. They start to chat. "How did it go today, good catch?" – "Couldn't have been better." – "Are you going back out?" – "No." – "Well, you could catch even more, sell more and make more money." – "And?" – "Then you could afford more and do everything you wanted to do!" – "Like, relaxing in the sunshine?"

One client shared how she never got past her favourite interiors shop without purchasing yet another candle or cushion, knowing full well that her home featured too many of these items already. Why was it impossible to resist? At some point she realised that she was trying get at something far more substantial when filling up another carrier bag. Her work schedule was so hectic that she never made time to relax, snuggle into an armchair and light a candle. The candles and cushions she kept buying were symbols of what she was currently missing most: peace and quiet.

Often we acquire an object as a stand-in for an underlying desire. Being human we long for security, we want to give and receive love, make a difference or contribute towards a greater good. Genetically ingrained needs for permanence and stability clash with an intrinsic desire for emotional and intellectual growth. Shifting our attention away from outside-wants helps to uncover the needs beyond. Is it about purchasing another whale song, birdsong, calming sound of waves, relaxation technique recording or figuring out a way how to end up with more me-time? Another movie, magazine, podcast subscription or spicing up our daily routine? As soon as we approach the desired essence and meet those longings directly, we stop trying to get there via the diversion of new stuff, reducing the risk of suffocating the inner campfire under heaps. Flames are starting to blaze up again when we shovel some clutter off the red heat and we might find ourselves going where we have wanted to go. *"Having a wild and whacky time in Lebanon. Have been way out of my comfort zone since I touched down in Beirut some days ago... Got myself this gadget to stay in touch with the rest of the world which is not bad for a non-techie like me."* This message was sent by a class regular in her fifties who used to go on local walking holidays before she got herself involved in the saga that is the clutter-clearing journey. Beware of adventures – no liability assumed for what gets kick-started by letting go of the first mug!

How many more times are we going to witness crocuses and snowdrops nudging their dinky heads out into the snowy cold, no longer able to resist the promise of spring? Forty times? Three times? Let's unfold with them into the glistening light of a new season. Let's get all big headed and sing in the dark.

Let's burn brighter than the sun.

Clutter hide-and-seek

Things are shape shifters. One minute they are perfectly useful and adored and when we look again they have transmogrified into clutter. Secretly, over night. They have flown under the radar and accomplished the impossible, escaped our eagle eye while flaunting themselves on the shelves. Clutter control is the name of the game, the mission to make out the suspects and indulge in a regular fix of clearing as you go. From now on, no object is safe. Everything can be summoned to undergo random clutter testing when we walk around pretending to be a shop assistant, picking up stuff to be reshelved or taken to the till (the front door volunteered to step in for that part) to leave for good. It only takes nineteen days to form a new habit!

Zillions of glorious accessories and gadgets out there wait for us to shop around the clock but even by the time we have run out of space we just own a tiny fraction. An alternative option is to delight in the consumerist wonders of this world as and when seen on others. Beauties in thing-format enrich our lives but there is no need to turn ourselves into bag ladies or gentlemen due to the 'must own this, must bag this, must carry this home' reflex.

The letting go starts way before we have become attached. Our new life of window shopping tastes of freedom and the unlimited potential of owning the world. Out and about we are cruising the open seas of the shopping mall, intoxicating ourselves with clothes, colours, gadgets, ideas and accomplishments – of others. We dive into street life and overdose on sounds, lights and scents of this interactive, multisensory art installation. When we notice an extraordinarily magnificent specimen we say it out loud, right into the face of the wearer, how gorgeous they look, how gorgeous they are, carving a smile into a face for the nanosecond of an eternal moment. We pour shivers down a spine and leave it at that. No more devaluing a compliment by the greedy follow-up, "Oh, by the way, where did you get those...?"

It does not come with a use-by-date but even music can go off, for our ears only. Tunes we once loved have suddenly lost the sound of music and hit our eardrums as noise or kitsch. Sounds are like taxis, they can take us places. Do we want to jump off the musical time machine in the distant past of 'teenagedom'? Or foray into territories unknown as a staff member of the couch crew, surfing sound waves to the spheres of beyond; being carried out of range of even the remotest of remote controls.

Our little blue planet rotates around its axis at over 1000 km/h, hurtling around the sun at 100,000 km/h. Our entire solar system whirls at a speed of a million km/h around its centre, the Milky Way. Little wonder that we are getting dizzy and have to hold on tight to our prefab de-accelerators made of paper, glass, wood, aluminium and plastic. Anchor ourselves in the safe gravity of wool, clay, steel, porcelain, cotton, elasthan and polyethylene, to name but a few. Otherwise, who knows, we might tumble off the edges.

Living life to the full

When a lack of energy grinds us into an almost-standstill, enthusiasm is no longer an option and even being remotely entertaining becomes a tall order. Enter a clearing technique that is such fun that it replaces frustration with delight before you can say instant coffee. It is about reintegrating the so-called 'good' stuff back into our life, resurrecting the exiles waiting for the infamous special occasion and free them from their dreary existence of rusting and generally rotting away. We seem to be in awe of funny bits like silver cutlery or crystal glasses and leave anything remotely beautiful untouched. Why use the fabulous stuff we own if we can drink from recycled chocolate spread jars. Candles had moved in, hoping to be lit one day, no such luck yet. And the dinner party never got past the planning stages.

One class member decided to get serious about one of the most pleasurable ways of clutter clearing and actually *use* the things that had been locked away for committing the offence of being too nice. She decided to get radical and take her best crockery out of the dresser where it was collecting dust while waiting for Christmas to come round again. She donated all mismatched plates and cups to charity and made space for the queen of dining sets. Now she treats herself to eating from decent china every single day. How amazingly sane is that?

Anything unused is life not lived. Welcome to the brave new world of clutter clearing fun where the concept of 'keeping for best' has been shredded, for good. We have unearthed the treasures to let them work their magic and transform any drab Tuesday into the unique fest it could be. The revolution starts at home; we write the shopping list with the most outrageously gold plated pen available (and chuck the gift box it came in). We dress up for going out – to the post office that is – who wants to be underdressed when they could be overdressed. Just when we are about to get down to business and unwrap a glass or put on that top with the label still on, our friend shows up. "You know I'm here to help. Listen, put that precious thing back. Think of the dangers: wear and tear! Stains! Cracks! If you want to be stubborn and insist on actually using this, the unspeakable could happen – disaster might strike with a breakage. Shattered into a thousand pieces, smashed, gone, forever. You wouldn't want that to happen, would you? So be a good girl/boy now and put it back." We draw a deep breath, take heart and reply defiantly, "Well it's only a bit of glass after all!" In an ideal world we are that brave. Catwoman, Batman, Supergirl and Lucky Luke rolled into one we decapitate fear with a triumphant roar, jump on the waiting horse and gallop off into the Promised Land clutching our best crockery. Fade out into the golden sunrise and vast wilderness of a clutter-free open prairie.

By Monday however, we are being good again. We deny ourselves any frivolous abundance and tug the slipcovers back over. – Who are we 'saving' stuff for? Ourselves, aged 95? The very old and the very young have got one thing in common – they know how to access happiness without stuff. We arrive with nothing, branch out, downsize and leave with nothing. If we insist on keeping the unused we might as well adopt the concept of the little one who said, "I'm going to save that for yesterday."

In case we are saving for generations to come, how do we know what they are after? It might be something wildly different from our tea set and table cloths hand-me-downs. They might be after a life without slipcovers, dusting or polishing. They might want to be walking on sunshine, oh yeah.

Fear has its place when it prevents us from falling off a cliff or being eaten by a lion. Once it oversteps its boundaries as a life-saver, it becomes a limiting emotion that prevents good things from happening. Best to put it away in a box, close the lid and run outside into the dewy grass or the midnight hours or the freezing cold and get on with living this one-off life to the full. Forget about the neighbours, overdo the exclamation marks and shout at the top of your lungs. "I know what strumming a guitar feels like!! I stroked a cat!! I raced downhill on bikes, skis, wheelchairs and a blown up tyre, I got carried away by camels and caramels!! Hitting the highs at high noon – been there done that, *everything is gonna be all-right!!*"

When we condemn our belongings to wait for a tomorrow that never comes we are in danger of joining them playing possum and carrying on waiting regardless. For a partner. For the relationship to swing back into being as happy as it never was. For the turning of the tide, for the pressure to ease off, for things to get easier. Waiting for a baby, for another child, for the kids to start school or finish university. For something to happen at work, a new job, a new home, the move. Waiting for the lunch break, the end of the working day, the end of working life. The weekend, the holiday, a sunny day. Spring, summer, snow, the evening, the morning, more time, more energy, more fun, a rest. The message, the call, the hit of the like button. For someone or something to come along and sprinkle fairy dust into our days to whizz away the drag. The delivery of assorted patent remedies and made-to-measure instructions manuals to finally pull it off – living this simplified, focused, cookie cutter fairy tale of a life.

Clearing unmasks the waiting game as missing of the moment and negation of life itself. Let's flourish in the Now and send flowers to the living instead of wilting wreaths that are delivered too late to make the recipient smile.

Here is a story. A friend of mine opened his wife's underwear drawer, picked up a silk paper wrapped box and said, "This is not an ordinary package." He unwrapped it and sat down, staring at the red silk paper. "She got this the first time we went to New York, eight or nine years ago. She has never put it on. She was saving it for a special occasion. Well, I guess this is it." He went to the bed and placed the gift box next to the other items of clothing he was taking to the funeral house. His wife had just died. He turned to me and said, "Never save anything for a special occasion. Every day in your life is a special occasion." I think those words have changed my life. Now I read more and clean less. I sit down sometimes, just looking around, without worrying about anything. I spend more time with my family and friends. I have understood that life should be an experience to be lived up to, not survived through. I no longer keep anything. The words *someday and one day* are fading from my dictionary. If it's worth seeing, listening or doing, I want to see, listen or do it *now*. Each day, each hour, each minute is special.'

Stop waiting. Start seeing, hearing, skipping, climbing, sobbing. Leaping and build your wings on the way down. Get up, listen, cry laughing. What does a day taste like that has the living daylight lived out of it? What does a moment sound like that is so full to the brim it is spilling over? What does an hour look like that has been squeezed for every last bit of zest? Launch the experiments into the stratosphere of possibility.

Life is what we decide to make it. We are free to use the years we have been given to accumulate and administrate stuff. We are free to make them about exploring what it means to be human, in all its glorious dimensions. The choice is ours.

The bank of life pays 86,400 units into our account every day. The deal: anything we do not spend within the 24-hour period expires. We might as well blow every single one of those seconds and waltz off with yet another experience.

A life without challenges, without change, untouched by grief or the fate of others – what would we do with such a life? Every encounter, every event gently steers us towards our purpose. We harvest the fruits of our labour with the power of hands and heart. Bread for body and soul.

May there be flowers in between the grains, a blossom opening up when we achieve something glorious; like finding a heart with a word of our love.

CLEAR OF CLUTTER
The Bagua

THE FENG SHUI BAGUA IS A GRID WHICH REVEALS HOW THE DIFFERENT AREAS OF ANY BUILDING/ROOM YOU OCCUPY ARE CONNECTED TO SPECIFIC ASPECTS OF YOUR LIFE.

Prosperity Wealth Abundance	Fame Reputation Illumination	Relationships Love Marriage
Elders Family Community	Health & Unity	Creativity Offspring Projects
Knowledge Wisdom Self-Improvement	Career Life Path The Journey	Helpful Friends Compassion Travel

TURN THE SHEET OF PAPER UNTIL THE ENTRANCE OF YOUR HOUSE/APARTMENT/ROOM IS PARALLEL TO THE LOWER EDGE OF THE SHEET — AS IF YOU ARE FACING TOWARDS IT AND ABOUT TO STEP INSIDE. AND THEN HAVE FUN DISCOVERING WHAT YOU TEND TO DUMP WHERE!